COFFEE

A Guide to Buying, Brewing and Enjoying

Revised Edition

KENNETH DAVIDS
Drawings by M. L. Duniec

101 PRODUCTIONS
San Francisco

Distributed to the book trade in the United States
by Charles Scribner's Sons, New York.

Published by 101 Productions
834 Mission Street
San Francisco, California 94103

Library of Congress Cataloging in Publication Data

Davids, Kenneth, 1937-
    Coffee, a guide to buying, brewing, and enjoying.

    Bibliography: p.
    Includes index.
    1. Coffee.   I. Title.
TX415.D38 1981   641.3'373   80-27222
ISBN O-89286-186-X

CONTENTS

INTRODUCING IT
The information gap; the perfect cup; specialty vs. commercial coffees

COFFEE DRINKERS are as in love with coffee as wine drinkers and pipe smokers with their habits, but maybe less aware of their infatuation. Who hasn't refused to give up some coffee-darkened eyesore of a cup, despite social pressures that would crumble Romeo or Juliet? There it stays, on the bottom shelf, messing up the effect of four feet of sparkling porcelain and glassware. "It's Freddie's favorite cup." This is plainly the stubbornness of love. When I ran a cafe I had customers who refused to give up their cups to the busboy—and they didn't want a refill either. They just wanted a cup sitting there to bring back memories, something to fondle now and then, until the aroma went away.

There are differences, however, between the average coffee lover and, say, a wine fancier. The wine lover first, knows a good deal about wine, or at least can talk a good deal about wine, and second, craves variety. One seldom is served the same wine twice when one goes to dinner at a wine fancier's house, whereas even people who pay attention to coffee tend to settle on one brand and one mode of preparation, and stay with it for years, morning after morning, night after night.

INTRODUCING IT

But along with everything else we do in the kitchen, coffee-drinking habits have been re-examined by kitchen fundamentalists, new-wave gourmets, and economy-priced jet-age cosmopolitans. Nearly every sizeable city has its growing quota of specialty coffee stores, usually with a "Coffee, Tea and Spices" sign outside and a lot of burlap decoration and fragrant stuff behind glass inside. Coffee drinkers are beginning to approach their beverage less as habit, and more as adventure.

a knowledge gap

There is a knowledge gap, however. When faced with an array of names reminiscent of a sixth-grade geography book, many a consumer will buy a pound of Colombian because he heard about it in some advertisement, take it home, pre-ground, and put the old one-and-a-half tablespoons in the pumping percolator. He's better off than he would be with a can of commercial coffee, but he has no more taken advantage of the possibilities of specialty coffee than a jug-wine drinker who randomly chooses his first bottle of varietal wine. Worse yet, the coffee adventurer may fall prey to Madison Avenue and sample one of the new exotic instant coffee mixes cluttering up the shelves (Instant Cappuccino, Instant Cafe a l'Orange, Instant Cafe a la Scam, etc.). He will most likely go directly back to regular grind in a can, and I don't blame him.

a practical book

It is to this knowledge gap, and the renewed interest in the variety and sensual pleasure to be got from coffee, that this book is addressed. It is not another gift cookbook filled with foreign exclamations and inedible recipes stolen from other cookbooks, recipes that you try once, during the week between Christmas and New Year. It *is* a practical book about a small but real pleasure, with real advice about how to buy better coffee, make better coffee, enjoy coffee in more ways, avoid destroying yourself with caffeine while drinking coffee, and, if you care to, talk about coffee with authority. Throughout, I've tried to blend the practical and experimental with the historical and descriptive, and produce a book simultaneously useful in the kitchen and entertaining in the armchair.

The present (relatively) high price of coffee is one more reason to approach the drink with love and respect. Coffee is high-priced only when compared to cheap tea. A cup of the world's finest coffee, for instance, costs less than the same amount of Coca-Cola, and is 10 or 15 times cheaper than a wine of similar distinction.

I used to stay at a little run-down hotel in Ensenada, Mexico, overlooking the harbor. The guests gathered every morning in a big room filled with threadbare carpets and magazine chromos of the Swiss Alps, to sit on broken-down couches, sip the hotel coffee, and look out at the harbor through some sagging French doors.

the perfect cup

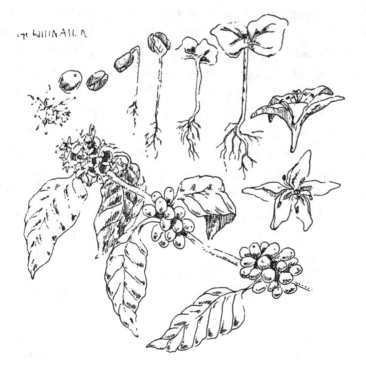

INTRODUCING IT

Nachita, the old woman who ran the hotel, made the coffee herself, from very cheap, black-roasted, sugar-glazed beans. I assume the beans were the carelessly picked and primitively processed type called "naturals" in the coffee trade, because the coffee had a certain rank bitterness associated with such beans, a taste which is never forgotten. Nachita's tendency to lightly boil the coffee didn't help much either. At any rate, by the time the coffee got to us it was dark, muddy, and sourly bitter, with a persistence no amount of sugar could overcome nor Carnation evaporated milk obscure.

By anyone's standards it was bad coffee. But—you can guess the rest—the morning, the sun on the sea, the chickens in the back yard, the mildewed smell of Nachita's carpets and the damp smell of old stone walls, the clumsy bilingual conversations, the glorious poems about mornings and Mexico I never put on paper, got mixed up with that sour bitterness and turned it into something more than perfect; I loved it. I even loved the tinny sweetness of the condensed milk. After all, there wasn't any other cup of coffee, and I was happy.

A cup of coffee is as much a moment caught in the matrix of time and space as it is a beverage; "perfect" cup of coffee to whom and when?

certain universals

Of course there are certain universals in good coffee making, which run through this book like comforting refrains: good water, good beans properly roasted and freshly ground, careful brewing, and so on, all of which fortunately do not depend on sleazily exotic mornings in Ensenada, and work even at five o'clock on rainy Sundays in Cleveland.

There is plentiful indication, for instance, that the steady decline in coffee drinking in the United States (the 38 gallons a year the average American drank 10 years ago has now shrunk nearer to 30 gallons) is owing to the widespread use of instant coffees which lack both flavor and aroma. Why else would the consumption of quality coffees be spectacularly increasing, while the consumption of commercial coffees continues to decrease?

Nevertheless, the consumer of the average tasteless, thin-bodied instant may be in for a bit of a surprise when he tastes his first cup of one of the world's great, rich, full-bodied coffees. If one gets used to living in a studio apartment, a mansion may feel a little uncomfortable—for the first week.

Furthermore, the best cup of Middle Eastern-style coffee, say, will taste like a cross between cough syrup and ice-cream topping to an American, while the Middle Easterner would probably use the contents of the American's Chemex to polish the buckles on his camel harness. Even with good coffee, tastes differ.

Coffee drinkers worldwide can be divided by habit and preference into three great traditions: first, the Middle East, second, southern Europe and Latin America, and third, North Americans, northern Europeans, and the rest of the pale-faced, English-speaking world.

three great traditions

Middle Easterners remain closest to basics. They like their coffee roasted dark, generally; grind it to a powder, generally; bring their coffee to a boil several times, always; and produce a small, bittersweet cup heavy with sugar and sediment. The little cups are sipped with a ceremonious air, at all times of the day, and nobody rushes.

The southern European or city-dwelling Latin American has two perfect cups, one for morning and one for afternoon and evening. He always prefers his coffee dark roasted, bitter, almost burned. He usually prefers it from an espresso machine, a big machine that dribbles out small amounts of strong, black, heavy-bodied brew, foamy on top, with a little, not a lot, of sediment in the cup. In the morning he mixes a stiff shot of this stuff with hot milk in a big bowl or tall, wide-mouthed glass, something he can really get his hands around. He wants to warm his palms and fill his nostrils with it, dip his roll in it; if he could, he'd probably take a bath in it. At night or in the afternoon, however, the southern European's perfect cup is as small as the Middle Easterner's, maybe one-fourth the size of his morning bowl, black, but just as strong and sweet.

The perfect cup of English-speaking coffee is at the furthest remove from the Middle Easterner's. First, beans roasted brown, not black, without a trace of the burned, bitter tang of Europe or the Middle East. The beverage must be clear (*no* sediment!), light, smooth, and so delicate milk or even sugar tends to overwhelm any pretense to body or flavor.

The typical North American neither immerses himself in big bowls every morning, nor saves his coffee for after dinner, nor takes quick little sips out of tiny cups with ceremonial deliberation. He drinks the stuff all day out of office urns, or carries a half-filled cup around while doing the housework. And as has often been pointed out, the North American's coffee is his beverage as well as his dessert; he not only finishes meals with it, he's liable to start and middle with it, too.

a fourth tradition

Finally, there is a fourth tradition which is dangerously close to swamping all the other three: dumping a spoonful of brown powder in a styrofoam cup of hot water and drinking it while walking out the door into the smog. This tradition has of late become well established in all parts of the world. A friend reports that she was unable to find anything except Nescafé in the cafés of Guatemala Antigua, the home of one of the world's finest coffees. The final blow, however, came in Guadalajara, where she ordered a cappuccino and watched in stunned silence as the counterman turned from the gleaming espresso machine to dump a spoonful of brown powder into a cup of foamed milk.

One reason for such a paradox, of course, is the fact that the best Mexican and Central American coffee is bought by the United States whereas the locals can only afford the cheapest grades of local coffee, and may prefer a decent instant instead. But I can't help but feel the reasons are more than economic; I'm sure instant coffee is part of the whole anti-sensual, compulsive work ethic of industrialism, creeping over the world like the shadow of a giant billboard. After all, instant makes for considerably shorter coffee breaks.

At any rate, readers of this book need not feel limited by any tradition. A cup of coffee like any other gesture can be enriched by choice and consciousness. The pages following offer you not the "perfect cup," but the perfect *cups*.

INTRODUCING IT

All the coffees I will be advising you to buy are known in the trade as "specialty" coffees. The opposite of specialty is "commercial" coffee. From the consuming end the most immediately noticeable difference between commercial and specialty coffees is packaging: Commercial coffee comes in little bottles of instant, or already ground and packed in a tin. Specialty coffee comes as whole beans, in either one-pound bags or in bulk, and needs to be ground before it's brewed.

Commercial coffee is usually roasted and packed in large plants, under nationally advertised brand names; specialty coffee is usually roasted in small stores or factories, using traditional methods and technology, and is often sold where it's roasted.

Specialty coffees offer considerably more choice than commercial coffees; you can buy coffee by the place the bean originated ("Kenya," "Colombian"); by roast ("French roast," "Italian roast "); or by blend designed for the time of day, price or flavor. Commercial coffees offer only a very limited selection of blend and roast, and little possibility whatsoever of buying straight, unblended coffees.

Specialty coffees offer more opportunity for the consumer to participate in the creation of his pleasure; commercial coffees are a *fait accompli* in a tin or bag.

The final, most important difference between commercial and specialty coffees is the way they taste and smell. The best commercial blended coffees are good. The worst are atrocious. But bought fresh and brewed correctly, specialty coffees are more than good; they are superb, and superb in a variety of ways. If you want to know how specialty coffees get to be better than commercial coffees, read on. If you take my word for it, skip to Chapter 2.

Coffee buyers divide the world's coffee production into three main categories: "high-grown mild," "Brazilian," and "robusta."

High-grown mild coffees demand the highest prices on the world

SPECIALTY VS. COMMERCIAL

WHY BUY SPECIALTY

11

INTRODUCING IT

high-grown mild

"Brazilian"

robusta

market. The coffee tree will not tolerate frost, but will not flourish when temperatures are extremely high either. This means coffee grows best in certain well-watered, mountainous regions of the tropics. High-grown mild coffees, no matter where they come from, are grown at altitudes over 2,000 feet above sea level, usually between 4,000 and 6,000 feet. They are also produced from berries that are picked only when ripe, and prepared with care. The responsible specialty coffee roaster uses only the finest high-grown mild coffees.

The use of the term "Brazilian" to describe the next most preferred group of coffees is misleading, since Brazil also produces excellent mild coffees. The trade term "Brazilian," however, refers to lower-grade coffees which are grown at low altitudes on vast plantations and mass harvested. These coffees at best have a middle-of-the-road, neutral flavor, with a flat aroma. Most decent commercial blends contain large proportions of "Brazilian," with smaller additions of high-grown milds.

Both "high-grown mild" and "Brazilian" coffees are produced from plants which belong to the botanical species *Coffea arabica.* The arabica is the original coffee plant; it still grows wild in Ethiopia, and was first cultivated in Yemen at the southern tip of the Arabian peninsula. *Coffea arabica* was then carried around the world by coffee-hooked devotées, much as European wine grapes spread to form the basis of the world's wine industry. All specialty coffees come from *Coffea arabica* stock, which still makes up the majority of the world's production.

Many other species of coffee tree grow wild in Africa, however, and one, the *Coffea robusta,* has grown to major importance in world markets. The main advantages of the robusta are its resistance to disease, and the fact that it will grow successfully at lower altitudes than *Coffea arabica.* The bean, however, does not have the fragrance or flavor of the best arabica, or even a decent Brazilian, and demands the lowest prices in the world market. Robusta is used as a component in the cheapest American commercial coffees, especially instant coffees.

The coffee bean, like all beans, is a seed; it grows at the heart of a small berry, about the size of the end of your little finger. Before the coffee can be shipped and roasted the bean must be separated from the berry. Nature has been particularly lavish in its protection of the coffee bean, and removing the three sets of skin and one layer of pulp from around the bean is a complex process. If done properly, the coffee looks better, tastes better and demands a higher price.

The worst preparation would be as follows: The coffee berries are stripped—leaves, unripe berries, and all—onto the ground. This mixture is then scooped up, sifted, dried in big piles, and some time later the hardened berry is stripped off the bean. Some beans will be small and deformed, shriveled, or discolored. In poorly prepared coffee all the beans, good and bad, plus a few twigs, a little dirt, and some stones, are shipped together. The various flavor taints associated with cheap coffee—earthiness, mustiness, harshness, and so on—derive from careless picking and drying.

the worst preparation

The best preparation would run like this: The beans are selectively picked as they ripen. The outer skin is immediately scraped loose, exposing the pulp. The beans are then soaked, and the sweet pulp fermented off the bean. More soaking, or more properly washing, follows, before the bean is dried and the last layers of skin, now dry and crumbly, are stripped off the bean. In some cases, the beans are further tumbled and "polished" to improve their appearance.

the best

Coffee is graded according to these three criteria: the quality of the bean (altitude and species), quality of preparation, and size of the bean. A fourth criterion is simply how good the coffee tastes and smells, what coffee people call "cup quality."

Again: The specialty coffee seller buys only the best grades of coffee, which means high-grown mild beans, excellent preparation, with high cup quality. When you buy from a responsible specialty coffee seller you should be buying top quality, no matter what country of origin or roast you choose.

KALDI & the DANCING GOATS

1 HOW IT STARTED
The odyssey of the bean

THE MOST FAMOUS version of the origin of coffee goes like this: Once upon a time in the land of Arabia Felix, lived a goatherd named Kaldi. Kaldi was a sober, responsible goatherd, whose goats were also sober, if not responsible. One night Kaldi's goats didn't come home, and in the morning he found them dancing in abandoned glee near a shiny, dark-leaved shrub with red berries. Kaldi soon determined that it was the red berries on the shiny, dark-leaved shrub that caused their eccentric behavior, and it wasn't long before he was dancing, too.

Finally a learned *innam* from a local monastery came by, sleepily, no doubt, on his way to prayer. He saw the goats dancing, Kaldi dancing, and the shiny, dark-leaved shrub with the red berries. Being of a more systematic turn of mind than the goats or Kaldi, the learned *innam* subjected the red berries to various experimental examinations, one of which involved parching and boiling. Soon neither the *innam* nor his fellows fell asleep at prayers, and the use of coffee spread from monastery to monastery, throughout Arabia Felix, and from there to the world. We never find out whether Kaldi and his goats dropped dead from exhaustion and caffeine poisoning, or learned to control their habit.

a sleepy monk

HOW IT STARTED

Owing to stories like this, coffee was first thought to have originated in what is now Yemen, on the Arabian peninsula, where Europeans first found it growing. But botanical evidence indicates *Coffea arabica* originated on the plateaus of central Ethiopia, several thousand feet above sea level, where it still grows wild, shaded by the enormous umbrella-like trees of the rain forest. How it got from Ethiopia to Yemen is uncertain. One guess is those "Arabian traders" who always seem to be schlepping things around in history books. Another possibility is the Persians, who during their leisurely invasions of Egypt and Yemen around the sixth century A.D. could have brought coffee with them from Ethiopia across the Red Sea to Yemen. At any rate, *Coffea arabica* seems to have been cultivated in Yemen from about the sixth century on. Black African cultures used coffee earlier, but as a solid food, combined with animal fat, for instance, or chewed like nuts.

In Arabia coffee was first mentioned as a medicine, then as a beverage taken in connection with meditation and religious exercises by dervishes. From there it moved into the streets and virtually created a new institution, the coffee house. Once visitors from the rest of the world tasted it in the coffee houses of Cairo and Mecca, the spread of *Coffea arabica* was, by 16th-century standards, electrifyingly rapid. The extraordinary story of the dissemination of *Coffea arabica* from the seed of possibly *one tree* to virtually the entire world is full of the sort of passion and sacrifice that must come from deeper springs than greed alone. Everywhere that people tasted coffee they wanted it, and went through extraordinary pains to bring some home with them.

The arabica plant's amazing odyssey was only possible because of its stubborn botanical self-reliance; it pollinates itself, which means mutations are much less likely to occur than in plants which have a light pollen and require cross-fertilization. Most differences in flavor between arabica beans are caused not so much by differences in the plants themselves, but by the subtle variations wrought by soil, moisture, and climate. The plant itself has remained extraordinarily true to itself through five centuries of plantings around the world.

At first the Arabs, jealous of their discovery, refused to allow fertile seed to leave their country, insisting that all beans be first parched or boiled. All this jealous care was doomed to obvious failure, however, and it was inevitable that someone, in this case a Moslem pilgrim from India named Baba Budan, should sneak some seeds out of Arabia. Legend says he bound "seven seeds" to his belly, and as soon as he reached his home hermitage, a cave in the hills near Chikamalagur in south India, he planted them and they flourished. In 1928, William Ukers reported in his encyclopedic work *All About Coffee* that the descendants of these first seeds "still grow beneath gigantic jungle trees near Chikamalagur," presumably keeping other hermits alert and praising Allah.

the seven seeds

From the descendents of the "seven seeds" coffee plants spread up and down mainland India. The French became interested, but their attempt to propagate coffee in southern France, near Dijon, failed because the tree does not tolerate frost. The more enterprising Dutch, however, carried plants from Malabar, in India, the descendents of the first "seven seeds" of Baba Budan, on to Java, where after some effort coffee growing was established on a regular basis.

It was at this point in our history that coffee made its debut as the everyday pleasure of noblemen and other Europeans rich enough to afford exotic luxuries. Coffee was available either from Mocha, the main port of Yemen, or from Java. Hence the famous blend of "Mocha-Java," which in those days meant putting together in one drink the entire possible world of coffee experience.

Now comes one of the most extraordinary stories in the spread of coffee, the "saga of the noble tree." Louis XIV of France, with his insatiable curiosity and love of luxury, was of course by this time an ardent coffee drinker. The Dutch owed him a favor, and managed, with great difficulty, to procure him a coffee tree. The tree had originally been obtained at the

the noble tree

Arabian port of Mocha, then carried to Java, and then, finally, back across the seas to Holland, where it was brought overland to Paris. As soon as Louis saw that tree his eyes lit up. He is said to have spent an entire day communing with it himself, before turning it over to his botanists. The first greenhouse in Europe was constructed to house the noble tree; it flowered, bore fruit, and became one of the most prolific parents in the history of plantdom.

This was in 1715. From that single tree, billions of arabica trees, including most presently growing in Central and South America, sprung. However, true to the kinky karma of coffee, the odyssey of the offspring of the noble tree was not easy or straightforward.

The first sprouts from the noble tree reached Martinique in the Caribbean in about 1720, owing to the truly heroic efforts of Chevalier Gabriel Mathiew de Clieu, who assuredly follows Baba Budan into the coffee hall of fame. De Clieu first had difficulties talking the authorities in Paris into giving him some trees (he finally stole them), but this was nothing to what he went through once at sea. First, a fellow traveler tried to rip up his trees, a man who, De Clieu writes, was "basely jealous of the joy I was about to taste through being of service to my country, and being unable to get this coffee plant away from me, tore off a branch." Other, more cynical commentators suggest the potential coffee thief was a Dutch spy bent on sabotaging the French coffee industry.

a coffee saboteur

Later, the ship barely eluded some pirates, nearly sunk in a storm, and was finally becalmed. Water grew scarce, and all but one of the precious little seedlings died. Now comes the most poignant episode of all: De Clieu, though suffering from thirst himself, was so desperately looking forward to coffee in the New World that he shared half of his daily water ration with his struggling charge, "upon which," he writes, "my happiest hopes were founded. . . . It needed such succor the more in that it was extremely backward, being no larger than the slip of a pink."

Once this spindly shoot of the noble tree reached Martinique, however, it flourished; 50 years later there were 18,791,680 coffee trees in Martinique, and coffee cultivation was established in Haiti, Mexico, and most of the islands of the Caribbean.

De Clieu became one of coffee's greatest heroes, honored in song and story. Pardon, in *La Martinique,* says he deserves a place in history next to Parmentier, who brought the potato to France. Esmenard, a writer of navigational epics, exclaims:

> With that refreshing draught his life he will not cheer;
> But drop by drop revives the plant he holds more dear.
> Already as in dreams, he sees great branches grow,
> One look at his dear plant assuages all his woe.

The noble tree also sent shoots to the island of Réunion, in the Indian Ocean, then called the Isle of Bourbon. This plant was found to be a somewhat different variety of arabica, with smaller beans, and was named *var. bourbon.* The famed Santos coffees of Brazil and the Oaxaca coffees of Mexico are said to be the offspring of the Bourbon tree, which by now had traveled from Ethiopia to Mocha, from Mocha to Java, from Java to a hot house in Holland, from there to Paris, from there to Réunion and eventually back halfway around the world to Brazil and Mexico. For the final irony, we have to wait until 1893, when coffee seed from Brazil was introduced into Kenya and Tanganyika, only a few hundred miles south of its original home in Ethiopia, thus completing a six-century circumnavigation of the globe.

variety Bourbon

Finally, to round out our set of coffee notables, we add the Don Juan of coffee propagation, Francisco de Melho Palheta of Brazil. The emperor of Brazil was interested in cutting his country into the coffee market, and in about 1727 sent De Melho Palheta to French Guiana, to obtain seeds. Like the Arabs and the Dutch before them, the French were jealously guarding their treasure, and Don Francisco, whom legend pictures as suave and deadly charming, had a hard time getting at those seeds. Fortunately for coffee drinkers, Don Francisco so successfully charmed the French Governor's wife that she sent him, buried in a bouquet of flowers, all the seeds and shoots he needed to initiate Brazil's billion-dollar coffee industry.

the Don Juan of coffee growing

2 BUYING IT
What the names mean; choosing coffee by roast

THIS IS THE CHAPTER with the essentials, so I'll try to keep my caffeine inspiration under control. Your first decision, of course, is where to buy your coffee. First, you can order by mail, which is at best an expedient and should only be indulged in if there are no specialty coffee suppliers in your town. Second, you can buy from a supermarket with a selection of whole-bean coffees and a do-it-yourself grinder. Third, you can buy from a "gourmet" food market or the fancy foods section of a large department store. Fourth, you can buy from a specialty coffee store.

The price may be lowest at the supermarket for all the well-advertised reasons: lower markup, brisker competition, higher volume. The same coffee at a specialty coffee store may cost up to 10 percent more, but you have many advantages: You can buy less than a pound at a time (a big advantage if you don't grind your own), request special blends, impress the clerk with your knowledge of coffee, sample new coffees, and wander around sniffing the aroma and staring at the little machines and gadgets. As for the third alternative, the gourmet food market or department store, whole-bean coffees found in such places are often excellent, but if sales volume is low and the manager disinterested, you may find yourself buying a stale coffee held too long on the shelf. Most stores specializing only in coffee, or in coffee and tea, care too much about their product to sell it less than fresh.

where to buy

Your next problem may be finding a specialty coffee store. Check the local yellow pages under "Coffee Sellers Retail"; if there are none, you could call supermarkets to see whether they handle whole-bean coffees, but most likely you'll have to limber up your writing fingers and check the back of this book for mail-order addresses.

Specialty coffee stores usually fall into one of the following categories:

- Roast their own coffee on the premises or nearby.
- As part of a chain, roast their own coffee at a central location.
- Buy their coffee from another local specialty roaster.
- Buy their coffee from several roasters.
- Buy their coffee green and have it roasted for them.

more exciting

To me stores falling into the first category are most exciting, and I suggest that in general you buy your coffee as close to the person who does the roasting as possible. The coffee will be fresher, often better, and the salesperson more informed.

And then, of course, you can visit shops and taste their coffee. Some specialty coffee stores, peculiar though it may sound, brew their coffee badly, so it's hard to tell anything about their beans from their samples. The biggest chain in Los Angeles, for instance, brews its coffee very weak in the morning and keeps it in thermos servers all day where it gradually loses what little flavor and aroma it started with. On the other hand, many specialty stores will brew *fresh* samples of their coffees to order for potential customers. The most common solution is to keep two coffees brewing at a time, and to rotate the choices.

from the same roaster

If no roasting machinery is in evidence, you might ask where the shop obtains its coffee. Half—maybe all—the stores in your area may get their coffee from the same roaster. A prominent San Francisco specialty roaster, for instance, sells his excellent coffee to supermarkets and specialty stores all over the San Francisco Bay Area, but his name seldom appears on the bag.

Of course even two shops that buy from the same supplier may differ in their handling of coffees. Staling begins the moment a coffee leaves the roasting machine, and a coffee sold by one shop a week after roasting will be significantly better than the same coffee sold elsewhere after three weeks. Look for well-established shops, large volume, and a proprietor who cares.

The typical coffee-specialty store has a row of glass-fronted cases or large glass jars where the coffees are displayed, and shelves and counters full of coffee makers, grinders, and other paraphernalia. Many are also "gourmet" shops selling specialty foods and cookware. Some are cafés or delicatessens as well as coffee stores. As for decor, most run to the budget, antique-country-store style: dark stained pine, coffee bags, brown tones.

In cities with large European neighborhoods, one occasionally finds stores or cafés where a few (sometimes only one) fine coffees are roasted and sold as they were before the victory of convenience foods and canned coffees. These places often produce the best in their line, though for a wide range of coffees and equipment you must go elsewhere.

Many stores carry as many as 30 varieties of coffee. Each one has a name, plus a few aliases. Take heart, however. No matter how many names there are, they all refer to either the degree to which the bean is roasted, the place the bean came from *before* it was roasted, or the dealer's name for a blend of beans.

ALL THOSE NAMES

Now look at the samples in the cases. You will notice that some are darker in color than others. You should also note that most names given these darker coffees are European, i.e., French, Italian, Viennese, continental, etc. These coffees are distinguished by the *length of time the bean is roasted*. Italian roast, for instance, is usually darker and has been roasted longer than Viennese. These names *do not* refer to the origin of the beans, however. Sometimes specialty coffee sellers specify the coffee which they have chosen to dark roast; in this case the coffee will be given a double-decked label like "Dark Roast Colombian" or "Italian Roasted Mexican." In most cases, however, the coffee a roaster chooses for his darker roasts will be an inexpensive blend of coffees from a variety of countries, and the name will refer only to the roast, not to the origin of the bean.

European names

Next to the coffees with European names, which will differ in color,

23

BUYING IT

you will note coffees which show the same light-to-medium brown color, and carry exotic, non-European names, like Sumatran, Kenya, or Mexican. Unlike the coffees with European names, these coffees are roasted about the same length of time, or to what the roaster considers typical "American" tastes. The difference here is not the roast, but *the origin of the bean itself.* A coffee labeled Sumatran, for instance, will consist entirely of beans from a single crop in a single country, Sumatra. Since coffee can only be grown successfully in or very near the tropics, such straight varietal coffees tend to carry names of an exotic and sultry timbre.

Straight coffees, in addition to the name of the country in which they originated, often carry qualifying names: "Guatemalan Antigua," "Kenya AA," "Java Arabica," "Colombia Plantation," and so on. Most of these qualifying terms are either grade designations ("AA"), or market names referring to coffee-growing regions ("Antigua"). A few, like "Arabica," describe a botanical species or variety, and epithets like "Plantation" or "Estate" indicate coffee grown on a large farm rather than peasant plots.

market names   I discuss market names at length in Chapter 3, under the countries to which they refer. There are literally thousands in the coffee trade, but fortunately only the most famous find their way into the vocabulary of the specialty coffee retailer. Some derive from the name of a district, province, or state; others from a mountain range or similar landmark; others from a nearby important city; and still others from the name of a port or shipping point. Oaxaca coffees from Mexico are named for the state of Oaxaca; the Kilimanjaro coffees of Tanzania for the slopes of the mountain on which these coffees are grown. The Harrar coffees of Ethiopia take their name from the old city of Harrar; the Santos coffees of Brazil from the name of the port through which they are shipped.

grade names   Retailers may also qualify coffee labels by grade name. Grading, of course, is a device for controlling the quality of an agricultural commodity so that buyer and seller can do business without personally examining every lot sold. Coffee-grading terminology is unfortunately varied and obscure:

every coffee-growing country has its own set of terms, and few are distinguished by their logical clarity. "Kenya AA" is an exception: Clearly "AA" is better than "A" or "B." But though the Colombian terms "excelso" and "supremo" are both clearly laudatory, one could hardly determine by the terms alone that "supremo" is the single highest grade of Colombian coffee, and "excelso" a more comprehensive grade consisting of a mixture of supremo and the less desirable "extra" grade. And although one may be aware that altitude is a prime grading factor in Central American coffees, one could hardly guess without coaching that "strictly hard bean" refers to Guatemalan coffees grown on plantations situated at altitudes of 4,500 to 5,000 feet, and "hard bean" 4,000 to 4,500 feet. The higher the altitude the slower maturing the bean, and the harder and denser its substance, hence "hard bean."

The average specialty coffee retailer's use of terminology in labeling his coffees is seldom logical or even consistent, even when dealing with straight coffees. Ideally one ought to be made aware of the country and region where the coffee originated, its grade, its botanical variety if relevant, and even the market name of the plantation or co-operative where it was grown or processed. The month and year it was harvested would also be helpful. But the retailer usually tacks, at most, one qualifying adjective onto the name of the country of origin and lets it go at that. Some retailers may choose the most significant qualifying adjective, others the most romantic, but the end result *most romantic* is still confusion. The reader who manages Chapter 3 should also manage the terminology fairly well, however, and at least be in a position to make intelligent deductions.

To find out how capable you are at this point of surmounting such confusion, try this: *Kenya.* A tropical name, therefore a straight coffee from Kenya, roasted medium brown to American tastes. *Kenya AA.* The qualifying adjective, AA, doesn't sound like a place, and has a superlative *a test* ring to it, so you figure it must be a grade. Of course, you're correct. *Sumatran Mandheling.* A tropical name, therefore a straight coffee from

Sumatra roasted medium brown; since Mandheling doesn't sound like a grade nor have you heard it mentioned as a botanical variety, you assume it is a market name referring to a specific coffee-growing region in Sumatra. You have deduced correctly. *Mexican Altura Coatepec.* Another straight coffee roasted medium brown, from Mexico. Coatepec sounds like a regional name; Altura has that superlative ring we associate with grades, and if you're at all familiar with Spanish you'll know it means heights, so you assume it's the name of a grade based on the altitude at which the coffee is grown. Correct. *French.* They don't grow coffee in France, so it must be a roast, darker than usual. Pick any prize on the lower shelf. *French-roast Mexican Oaxaca Pluma.* First of all a straight coffee from Mexico roasted more darkly than usual. Since Oaxaca is a city in Mexico, you figure (correctly) that Oaxaca refers to the region in Mexico where the coffee was grown. That leaves Pluma, which must be either a botanical variety or a grade; you guess grade and you're right. Any prize on the top shelf, including the pandas.

Deduction is even more in order when one begins to deal with blended coffees. Blends, of course, are mixtures of two or more straight coffees.

blended coffees There are two reasons to blend beans: one is to make a coffee with a flavor that is either better and more complete, or at least different from the flavor produced by a straight coffee. The other is to cut costs while producing a palatable drink.

Nearly all commercial coffee sold in cans or bags is blended. Commercial roasters might want to market a Kenya, for instance, but they can't be sure enough of an adequate supply of the same coffee month after month to warrant the promotional expense in getting a name accepted by the public.

With many blends found in specialty coffee shops the name gives us some clue as to the origin of the coffees involved. The simplest to interpret is the famous mixture of one-third Yemen Mocha and two-thirds Java Arabica, the "Mocha-Java" of tradition. Such a blend is not designed to save money, but rather to blend two coffees that complement one another: Yemen Mocha is a sharp, distinctive, medium-bodied coffee, whereas Java is smoother, deeper-toned, and richer. Together the two coffees make a more complete beverage than either one on its own.

Other blends are named after the dominant straight coffee and combine a cheaper neutrally flavored coffee with a more expensive "name" coffee. Thus we have "Jamaica Mountain Blend," or "Mocha Blend." The characteristics of the name coffee will still come through, less intensely than in a straight coffee, but distinctive enough if the blending is done right, and at a savings to the consumer. In other cases, the blender may use lesser-known coffees to mimic the characteristics of a more famous and hard-to-get or expensive coffee; thus we have "Jamaica *Style*" coffee, or "Kona *Style* Blend."

Another tendency in blend nomenclature might be called the generally geographical. We find a "Central American Blend," or a "Caribbean Blend." Or we meet blends named for the time of day we presumably might drink them: "Breakfast Blend" usually means a blend of brisk, lighter-bodied coffees roasted more lightly than "After-Dinner Blends," which are usually made up of heavier-bodied coffees carried to a darker roast.

generally geographical

In some cases, the seller may offer the very same blend roasted differently, giving it another name every time he carries the roast a few degrees darker. (For clues on solving this one, read the discussion of roasts.)

At this point we reach the ultimate test: the mysteriously named house blends, the beloved children of the proprietor or roaster, baptized with names of his personal fantasy. A specialty roaster may have one such child or a dozen. Some of these offspring may have been a tradition in a coffee-roasting family for a couple of generations; others may have been born yesterday; a few may be in detail at least unique; but most are standard blends well known in the coffee business, with slightly different proportions and fanciful names. Occasionally the name gives us a clue as to content, but most often we're faced with the arbitrary romance of the proprietor, whose preferences may run from mountaineering ("Tip of the Andes Blend"), to the elegantly British ("Mayfair"), to the darkly Latin ("Orsi").

mixed feelings   I confess to mixed feelings about all vaguely named blends. Romance and imagination are marvelous qualities and should be encouraged, but I also think the consumer deserves to be informed in a direct and unpatronizing way. I would prefer a little explicit description along with the imagination, just a line or two about origins and proportions. But for now, one can only ask questions and taste, which is excellent advice anyhow, regardless of how explicit the label.

A last few terms that are particularly ambiguous: "Turkish" coffee refers neither to coffee from Turkey nor roast: The name designates *grind* of coffee and *style* of brewing. "Turkish" is a common name for a medium- to dark-roasted coffee, ground to a powder, sweetened, boiled and served with the sediment still in the cup. "Viennese" is a slippery one. It can mean a somewhat darker-than-normal roast, or a *blend* of *roasts* (about half dark and half medium), or, in Great Britain, a blend of coffee and roast fig. "New Orleans Coffee" is usually a dark-roasted coffee mixed with chicory root, occasionally a dark-roasted Brazilian blend *without* the chicory.

Decaffeinated, or caffeine-free coffees, have had the caffeine soaked out of them; they are sold to the roaster green like any other coffee. Roasters in most metropolitan centers will offer both a medium or American roast and a dark-roast decaffeinated bean. The provenance of the bean should still be designated: "Decaffeinated French-roast Colombian," for instance. Some roasters may carry as many as five or six decaffeinated straight coffees. The epithet "water-only" applied to decaffeinated coffee means the caffeine has been removed from the bean without the use of a solvent.

In about 1978 an insidious fad crept off the instant food shelves and slunk over into the specialty coffee section: This aberration is the "flavored" whole-bean coffee. Typically either an inexpensive blend of beans or one of the less pricey Colombian coffees is sprayed with essential oils or other natural flavorings immediately after roasting, while the bean is cooling. The flavorings are absorbed into the bean. At this writing consumers are flocking into the stores requesting "chocolate-rum coffee," "chocolate-mint coffee," or a dozen other flavors, presumably to serve with their Thunderbird wine. I wish I could say this mutant came crawling out of Lake Mead into Las Vegas, but apparently it surfaced in New York, where at least some people should know better.

But to cut the snobby jokes and try to be helpful, if you buy any of these idiocies, try the chocolate. Avoid rum and brandy in particular; they taste decent when they're very fresh but develop the most rancid flavor imaginable when they're held on the shelf.

Given a good quality bean, roasting is probably the single most important factor influencing the taste of coffee. The significant variable is the length of time the coffee is roasted. The longer the roasting, the darker the bean. The darker the bean, the more tangy and bittersweet the flavor. When this flavor settles onto the average coffee drinker's palate, he calls it "strong."

Now for our first plunge into the taste jungle, unarmed except for a dictionary. "Strength" in coffee properly refers to the proportion of coffee to water, not the flavor of the bean. The *more* coffee and the *less* water the *stronger* the brew. So you could make a light-roasted, mild-flavored coffee very *strong,* and brew a dark-roasted, sharp-flavored coffee very *weak.*

I would rather call this dark-roasted flavor "dark," "bittersweet," "tangy," "sharp," or maybe "European." Anything but "strong," since we need that word for later. This flavor comes in degrees, depending on how dark the bean is roasted, and eventually becomes virtually a new flavor when the bean is roasted entirely black. To understand the chemistry behind the change, one needs to know what happens when a coffee bean is roasted.

the dark-roasted flavor

The green coffee bean, like all the other nuts, kernels, and beans we consume, is a combination of fats, proteins, fiber and miscellaneous chemicals. The aroma and flavor that make coffee so distinctive is present only potentially until the heat of roasting simultaneously forces much of the moisture out of the bean, and draws out of the base matter of the bean fragrant little beads of a volatile, oily substance variously called coffee

fragrant beads

essence, coffee oil, and coffeol. This stuff is not properly an oil, since it (fortunately) dissolves in water. Beside dissolving in water, it evaporates easily, absorbs other less desirable flavors readily, and generally proves to be as fragile a substance as it is tasty. Without it there's no coffee, only sour brown water and caffeine, yet it constitutes only one two-hundredth of the weight of the bean.

The roasted bean is in a sense simply a dry package for this oil. In light or American-roasted coffee, the oil gathers in little pockets throughout the heart of the bean. As the bean is held in the roaster for longer periods and more moisture is lost, the oil is further developed, and begins to rise to the surface of the bean, giving the characteristic oily appearance of darker roasts.

Beneath the oil the hard matter of the bean develops a burned flavor, which adds the bittersweet undertone so attractive to dark-roast aficionados. Eventually, the bean virtually turns to charcoal and tastes literally burned; this ultimately roasted coffee is variously called dark French, Italian, or heavy roast, and has an unmistakable charcoal tang.

Darker roasts also contain considerably less acid and somewhat less caffeine than lighter roasts; these too go up the chimney with the roasting smoke. Consequently, dark roasts lack that slightly sour snap or bite coffee people call "acidy." Some dark-roast coffees taste bitter or sour, but this is owing to the cheaper coffees used in the blend rather than the roast, and such sourness should not be confused with either the dry snappy bite of a good acidy coffee, or the bittersweetness of a good dark roast.

Back to terminology for a moment. Coffee drinkers are so habitual that whole nations march from coffee initiation to grave knowing only one roast. This peculiar uniformity accounts for the popular terminology for describing roasts: French roast and Italian roast, which vie for the darkest; Viennese or light French, a slightly darker roast than American; and so on down to what we might call "American roast," which is by country lightest of all.

This assigning of national names to coffee roasts is a bit arbitrary, but based on sound fact that southern Europeans roast their coffee darker than

1	Light brown; dry surface.	Cinnamon New England Light	Tastes more like toasted grain than coffee, with distinct sour or acidic tones.
2	Medium brown; dry surface.	Regular American Medium high Medium Brown	For an American the characteristic coffee flavor; the grain flavor is gone; a definite acidy snap, but richer toned and sweeter than 1.
3	Slightly darker brown; patches of oil on the surface.	Light French High Viennese* City Full city	A slight, dark-roasted, bittersweet tang, almost indistinguishable. Less acidy snap than 2.
4	Dark brown; oily surface.	Italian Espresso European** French After-dinner Continental Dark	A definite bittersweet tang; all acidy tones gone.
5	Very dark brown, almost black; very shiny, oily surface.	Dark French French Italian Heavy	Burned or charcoal tones plus the bittersweet tang; all acidy tones gone.

*Viennese also sometimes refers to a blend of about one-third dark-roasted beans (4 or 5), and about two-thirds medium-roasted beans (2).

**European sometimes refers to a blend of about two-thirds dark-roasted beans (4 or 5), and one-third medium-roasted beans (2).

northern Europeans or Americans. Whether the darkness of roast has some correlation to the relative intensity of nocturnal habits among the various nations of coffee drinkers, I'll leave to those who may want to consider this question over their second cup of dark-roast coffee.

names for roasts

The common terms for roasts among most coffee sellers are the standard, unnamed American roast (medium brown), Viennese or light French (slightly darker than American with the merest undertone of dark tang), Italian, espresso, or continental (dark brown, definitely dark flavored and bittersweet), and Italian or dark French (nearly black).

Your best bet is to learn to associate flavor with the color and appearance of the bean rather than with the name alone, but for reference I've condensed everything you'll need to know about the names of roasts in a table on the preceding page.

blending roasts

You can either buy a coffee roast as dark as you care to drink it, or make a blend of roasts. If you wish to blend roasts, buy a good, straightforward, acidy coffee like a Colombian, medium-roasted. Then begin adding French- or Italian-roasted beans, a few at a time, every time you grind yourself some coffee. Eventually, adding and subtracting, you'll arrive at proportions that please you and you can mix up your own blend, a half-pound at a time. Of course you may be the mercurial type who likes a different blend every time, in which case, carry on.

the next step

If you don't have a grinder, have the coffee-store clerk make a blend for you before grinding. I'd suggest you start with half dark-roast (the darkest) and half American-roast Colombian, and work the proportions up or down from there. The next step in determining your personal blend is to experiment with the light-roasted coffee; substitute some winey Kenya or heavy-bodied Sumatran for the Colombian, for instance. But for that, read on.

At this point a reader with a logical turn of mind might ask: Why don't specialty stores offer a whole line of dark-roasted straight coffees? Dark-roasted Colombian, for instance, dark-roasted Sumatran, and so on. A few coffees cannot be successfully dark-roasted; the bean is too soft and will become brittle and break apart if carried to too high a roast. Most coffees *can* be dark-roasted, and some roasters do offer a variety of dark roasts. Most do not, however. They argue that since dark roasting burns out many acids and other chemicals, with them go the subtle differences in flavor which distinguish one straight coffee from another. Thus it wouldn't be worth a specialty coffee roaster's effort to dark roast a variety of beans.

It is true that virtually all distinctions in flavor are burned out with a very dark, black-roasted preparation. But with the medium-dark roasts from categories 3 and 4 (see page 31), certain distinctions remain. Dark-roasted Kenya may not taste like Kenya anymore, but it will taste different from dark-roasted Colombian. Heavy-bodied coffees make heavy-bodied dark roasts, for instance. Some coffees dark-roast sweeter than others. Mexican, for example, makes a particularly sweet dark roast.

Also, roasters have different tastes in assembling their dark-roasted blends. Latin Americans, for instance, like a hint of sourness in their blends; it reminds them of the coffee their mamas made. So most dark-roasted coffees blended "for the Latin American taste" have a touch of the medicinal flavor called "Rioy." The same holds true for "authentic" New Orleans coffee, and some traditional, dark-roasted Italian espresso blends.

Once you learn to distinguish between roasts, you may want to pick out a dark-roasted *blend* which suits you best. Ask the clerk whether the dark-roast coffee he has for sale is a straight coffee or a blend. If it's a blend it may range from bitter to almost sweet, depending on the tastes of the *bitter to almost sweet* blender. The bitterness I'm describing here, of course, is a different matter entirely from the distinctive tang that comes from roasting coffee darkly in the first place. It is a quality of the coffee itself, rather than a flavor acquired through roasting.

And if you love dark-roasted coffee, in fact, if you love any kind of coffee, you may want to learn to roast your own. You can buy the best beans, roast them precisely to your taste, drink exquisitely fresh coffee always, and save considerable money.

3 TASTING IT
What to taste for;
choosing coffee by country
and market name

L EARNING TO DISTINGUISH roast is the first, relatively simple step in learning to taste and buy coffee intelligently. Once we move from roast to distinguishing coffees by country of origin, we enter a more ambiguous realm. Signs and brochures bombard us with light and full bodies, mellow, acidy, bright, and distinctive flavors, rich and pungent aromas, and on into the mellow, full-bodied tropical sunset. The bright-eyed assurance with which these terms are delivered shuts up everyone but people from Brooklyn and small children.

Most stores carry 15 to 30 varieties of straight coffee, all of which have to be described somehow or other on a sign or brochure. By the middle of the list you sense a certain strain; by the end the writer sounds desperate: "stimulating and vibrant," writes one; "an exotic coffee with a lingering aftertaste, full-bodied and provocative," writes another; "stands apart in its own special way," adds still another. Perhaps. Is the emperor wearing his new clothes? Do these coffees really taste different?

coffee brochurisms

They do. Differences stand out on a coffee-educated palate as clearly as sugar and salt. Experienced coffee tasters can distinguish the origin of most coffees in a blend simply by smelling and tasting. The problem is two-fold, and has to do with communication. First, the public doesn't understand coffee language, in other words, doesn't associate terms in the brochures with sensations in the mouth. Second, in their effort to make every coffee sound absolutely different from every other coffee, brochure writers often resort to mealy-mouthed romanticisms and gourmet-magazine clichés in place of genuine description.

The comedian George Carlin once pointed out there is no name for the two little ridges under the nose. The world is full of unnamed phenomena, and the closer we get to the heart of what it means to be alive, the more unnameable things get. The subtle differences in flavor and aroma among coffees are as palpable as breathing, but if anything, seem too real to be easily named. One slings a word at a flavor and feels like a painter trying to copy a sunset with a tar brush. So we're back to the same old refrain: The only thing to do is taste.

TASTING IT

Coffee tasting is in many ways more crucial to buying quality coffee than wine tasting is to buying quality wine. The reason: Wine is labeled very specifically, whereas coffee is labeled vaguely. For instance, we can learn from its label that a given wine is from France, a country; from Beaujolais, a region; and from Moulin-à-vent, a village in Beaujolais whose vineyards produce a particularly sturdy and rich red wine. Finally, the bottle tells us what year the grapes were grown and the wine bottled. Suppose, however, that one buys a coffee from Ethiopia. More than likely it will simply be labeled "Ethiopian." This tells us absolutely nothing, and would be analogous to simply labeling all wines from France, from the cheapest *vin ordinaire* to an aged Lafite-Rothschild, as "French."

limits of labels Some specialty roasters might go further and label a coffee "Ethiopian Harrar." Harrar, like Beaujolais, is a region, so we're getting closer, and "Harrar" further indicates it is a wet-processed, plantation-grown coffee. But even the fanciest specialty roaster will not tell us more. We are seldom told what plantation or estate or cooperative or village a coffee comes from, even though this last may be the most important piece of information of all. Nor are we told how long the coffee has been held in warehouses before roasting.

So a wine book can be much more specific in its recommendations than can a coffee book, first because wine labels are themselves more specific, and second, because coffee demands a closer collaboration from retailer and consumer, all the way from delivery in this country to the point of actually being drunk. A bottle of wine can certainly be affected by how it is stored, transported, and handled, but the fact remains it is packaged and ready to be enjoyed (at however remote a date) when it leaves the winery. But coffee is subject to three crucial operations—roasting, grinding, and brewing—by parties who are thousands of miles away from the tree where the bean originated. Thus, a Mexican Oaxaca Pluma even from the same crop and plantation may taste different after having been subject to the tastes of different roasters, and a variety of grinding and brewing methods. Coffee casts the consumer in a more active, and possibly more satisfying, role than does wine, but frustrates those who might prefer memorizing to tasting.

wine vs. coffee labels

Consequently, we must learn to taste. And when you move your trade to a new store, you should start tasting all over again, since your favorites may no longer be your favorites. Naturally, this only applies to stores who roast their own or obtain their coffee from different roasters. If you just move across town you may find you're buying from the same roaster, but under a different label. Perhaps I should say, ask questions first, and then start tasting.

taste again

There is no coffee-tasting ritual for the lay coffee drinker as there is for the wine drinker. Professional coffee tasters slurp it off a spoon, roll it around in their mouth, and spit it into a bucket, which isn't common after dinner behavior. I suggest when you're tasting you make coffee in your ordinary way, sample the aroma, taste a little black, and then, *drink* it. The professional taster is checking for defects as well as strengths of many coffees each day, whereas you simply want something that tastes good to you the way you drink it.

TASTING IT

However, you may well want to compare some samples of various coffees at the same sitting so you have some idea of what coffee terminology actually describes. Remember that dark-roasting mutes or eliminates distinctions in flavor, so make certain you sample coffees that have been roasted to standard North American taste: light- to medium-brown. You'll have to either make some individual samples with a small pot or a one-cup filter cone, or else brew it the way professional tasters do. In either case, you want to use the same amount of each coffee, ground the same, and brewed identi-

tasting the
professional way

cally. If you want to go professional, assemble a clean cup or shallow glass for each coffee to be sampled, a soup spoon, preferably silver plate, a glass of water in which to rinse your spoon between samplings, and something to spit into. Put one standard measure (two level tablespoons) of each coffee to be sampled, freshly and finely ground, in each cup; pour five ounces of near-boiling water over each sample. Part of the grounds will sink to the bottom of the cup, and part will form a crust on the surface of the coffee. At this point you will test each sample for aroma. Take the soup spoon, and leaning over the cup, break the crust. Virtually stick your nose in the coffee, forget your manners, and *sniff*. The aroma will never be more distinct than at this moment. If you want to sample it a second time, lift some of the grounds from the bottom of the cup to the surface, and sniff again.

After you've broken the crust most of the grounds should settle to the bottom of the cup. Use your spoon to scoop up whatever remains floating on the surface and dump it into your ad hoc spittoon. Now take a spoonful

suck it violently

of each coffee, lift it to a point just below your lips, and suck it violently into your mouth. Your purpose is to spray coffee all over your tongue in order to experience a single, comprehensive jolt of flavor. If you do it right you'll produce a loud, hissing jet-stream sort of noise, which will probably startle your cat but make your dog look friendly.

This spraying activity should give you a notion of flavor. Now roll the mouthful of coffee around your tongue, bounce it, chew it even. This exercise should give you a notion of both the body and acidity of your sample, concepts which I will attempt to define in a page or two. After all this—spit the coffee out. Continue this procedure until you can distinguish the qualities I discuss in the pages following. If your palate becomes jaded or confused, sip some cold water or eat a bit of bread.

In the following chart you will find listed most of the straight coffees you will encounter in American specialty coffee stores. There are five lists. *flavor families* Each of the first three represents a family of coffees, the fourth combines a couple of loners, and the fifth gives some special categories under which straight specialty coffees are often sold. First are the Latin American coffees, characterized by a bright, brisk acidity and clean, straightforward flavor. The second list is the Arabian and African family of coffees, characterized by a distinctive winey acidity. Third are the coffees of the Malay Archipelago plus China Yunnan, which have both heavy body and a lower-toned, richer acidity. In each list I've put the most distinctive and famous coffees first. The fourth list puts a pair of coffees together which have nothing in common except their difference from all the other coffees of the world, and the fifth gives some categories of coffees distinguished by factors other than geography.

When you begin tasting I suggest you choose one coffee from each of the first three lists, if possible Mexican Coatepec or Oaxaca Pluma, Ethiopian

Latin American family	Nicaraguan	Celebes
Jamaican Blue Mountain	Ecuador	or Sulawesi Kalossi
Guatemalan Antigua		China Yunnan
and Coban	*Arabian and African family*	Java Arabica
Colombian	Yemen Mocha	New Guinea
Costa Rican	Kenya	
Mexican Coatepec	Ethiopian Harrar	*Individualists*
and Oaxaca Pluma	Tanzania	Hawaiian Kona
Venezuelan Maracaibo	Uganda Bugishu	Indian Mysore
Peruvian Chanchamayo		
Brazilian Bourbon Santos	*Indonesian and*	*Some special categories*
Haitian	*New Guinea family*	Maragogipe
El Salvador	Sumatran Mandheling	Peaberry
Dominican Republic	or Ankola	Aged coffees
or Santo Domingo		

TASTING IT

Harrar, and Sumatran Mandheling. After you've made up three cups, begin smelling and tasting. You should eventually attempt to distinguish the following qualities:

acidity

Acidity: Taste those high, thin notes, the dryness the coffee leaves at the back of your palate and under the edges of your tongue? This pleasant tartness, snap, or twist is what coffee people call "acidy." It should be distinguished from "sour," which in coffee terminology means an unpleasant sharpness. The acidy notes should be very clear and bright in the Mexican, a little softer and richer in the Sumatran, and overwhelming in the Ethiopian Harrar. Aged coffees, and some coffees from Venezuela, Tanzania, and India, have little acidity and taste almost sweet.

An acidy coffee is somewhat analogous to a dry wine. In some coffees that "acidy" taste actually does become distinctively "winey"; the winey aftertaste should be very clear in the Ethiopian Harrar.

body

Body is the sense of heaviness, richness, thickness at the back of the tongue when one swishes the coffee around one's mouth. The coffee is not *actually* heavier, it just tastes that way. To introduce a wine analogy again: Burgundies and certain other red wines are heavier in *body* than clarets and white wines. In this case wine and coffee tasters use the same term for about the same phenomenon. The Ethiopian Harrar should definitely have the lightest body, and the Sumatran the heaviest, with the Mexican in the middle. If you can't distinguish body, try pouring milk into each. Note how the flavor of the heavy-bodied Sumatran carries through the milk, while the flavor of the Ethiopian dies away. If you do drink your coffee with milk, you should definitely buy a heavy-bodied coffee. If you're a black-coffee drinker you *may* (not always) prefer a lighter-bodied variety.

aroma

Aroma can't, strictly speaking, be separated from acidity and flavor. Acidy coffees smell acidy, and richly flavored coffees smell richly flavored. It is true, however, that some coffees, Colombian and Kona for instance, are more fragrant than others.

Flavor is the most ambiguous term of all. Acidity has something to do with flavor, and so do body and aroma. Some coffees simply have a fuller, richer flavor than others, whereas in others the acidy tang, for instance, tends to dominate everything else. One can also speak of a "distinctively" flavored coffee, a coffee whose flavor characteristics stand out in a crowd. Of the three coffees I suggested you sample, the Ethiopian is probably the most distinctive, the Mexican least distinctive, and the Sumatran the richest.

flavor

You will find many other epithets applied to flavor. "Mild" or "mellow" for instance. Mild-flavored coffees are usually low on acidity, but full-bodied and flavorful enough to be pleasant rather than bland. "Mild" is also used as an antonym to "harsh." Harshly flavored coffees are unpleasantly bitter, sharp, or irritating. There are also specialized coffee tasting terms to describe undesirable flavor characteristics: grassy, earthy, hidy, barnyard fermented, and so on. Presumably all the coffees you will be tasting will be superior, hence free from such defects.

The finest Mexican coffees come from the south of Mexico, where the continent narrows and takes a turn to the east. The state of Oaxaca occupies the western slopes of the central mountain range, and Veracruz the eastern. Fine coffees are produced in both states. The fine estate-grown coffees of Veracruz, particularly the best of those known as Altura ("High") Coatepec, are considered the best coffees produced in Mexico. The best washed coffees of Oaxaca State, Oaxaca and Oaxaca Pluma, run a close second. Other Veracruz coffees of note are Altura Orizaba and Altura Huatusco.

COFFEE BY COUNTRY

MEXICAN
Oaxaca Pluma, Coatepec

Don't expect any of these coffees to taste like the Mexican coffee you may have tasted while visiting rural Mexico, however. The brew most Mexicans drink is made from the natural or dry-processed coffees which have been passed over by the exporters; these cheaper beans are usually dark roasted and glazed with sugar. They make a sweet, heavy brew with a peculiar sour twist, which some visitors love and which turns others into temporary tea drinkers. If you have acquired a taste for such coffees, you must pursue it outside the confines of the specialty coffee store. Look for canned coffees from the southern United States, or coffees with Latino names sold in Puerto Rican, Mexican, or Cuban markets.

But the fine coffees of Mexico are a different matter. They are not among the world's greatest coffees, because they often lack richness and body, but at their best they are analogous to a good light white wine—delicate in body, with a pleasantly dry, acidy snap. If you drink your coffee black, and like a light, acidy cup, you will like the best Mexican coffees.

GUATEMALAN
Antigua, Coban

Guatemala's central highlands produce some of the world's best and most distinctively flavored coffees. The names to look for are "Antigua," from the countryside west of the old capital of Guatemala Antigua, and "Coban," from Alta Vera Paz, a district a hundred or so miles northeast of Antigua. Some shops may advertise their Guatemalan coffees by grade; the highest grades are "strictly hard bean," indicating coffees grown at altitudes of 4,500 feet or higher, and "hard bean," indicating those grown between 4,000 and 4,500 feet.

Both Antigua and Coban have a very distinct spicy, or better yet, smoky flavor which sets them apart from all other coffees. They are very acidy, and the spiciness or smokiness comes across as a twist to the acidy tones. In body, the finest Guatemalan coffees are medium to full, and rich in flavor. You will like Guatemalan coffees, especially Antigua, if you like their smoky, distinctive flavor, and a fairly rich cup.

EL SALVADOR

El Salvador, a tiny country which grows practically nothing but coffee, presents a problem for romantic writers of coffee brochures. The general consensus is that El Salvador coffee has a flavor somewhere between "neutral" and "mild." Someone else calls it "slightly sweet," which is about the most positive thing I've ever heard about it. I'd say it has a decent body but lackluster flavor. The best grade: "strictly high grown."

A coffee for the silent majority.

Central America

MEXICO

MEXICO CITY   JALAPA
COATEPEC   ⊙VERA CRUZ
HUATUSCO
ORIZABA

OAXACA PLUMA
⊙OAXACA
OAXACA PLUMA

COBAN
HONDURAS
GUATEMALA
GUATEMALA   EL
CITY   SALVADOR
ANTIGUA
EL SALVADOR

JINOTEGA
MATAGALPA
NICARAGUA
⊙MANAGUA

TRES RIOS
TARRAZU
SAN JOSE⊙
COSTA
RICA
PANAMA

TASTING IT

NICARAGUAN
Jinotega, Matagalpa

Nicaraguan presents still another challenge for coffee describers. One brochure tells us it's like Mexican, but different. In general I find it as middle of the road as Salvador: decent, straightforward flavor, fairly acid, with medium to light body. The districts of Jinotega and Matagalpa produce the best-known Nicaraguan coffees.

A coffee for Dodge Dart fanciers.

COSTA RICAN
Tres Rios, Tarrazu, Heredia, Alajuela

Costa Rican is a classically complete coffee; it has everything and lacks nothing. The best displays an exceptionally full body and robust richness. Good Mexican coffees are brisk; good Costa Rican coffees hearty.

Costa Rican coffee is grown primarily in the countryside surrounding the capital, San José. Four of the most famous coffees by district are Tres Rios, Tarrazu, Heredia, and Alajuela. Altitude may be a more important factor in determining flavor than district; "strictly hard bean" indicates a Costa Rican coffee grown above 3,900 feet; "good hard bean" 3,300 to 3,900. But again, don't become absorbed in names and grades. If the coffee you taste is rich and hearty, analogous to a good Burgundy, and you like it, it is a good Costa Rican coffee.

JAMAICAN
Blue Mountain, High Mountain

Jamaican coffee is a story of extremes; the lowland coffees of Jamaica are so ordinary they are seldom sold in the United States except as fillers in cheap blends; on the other hand Jamaica's highland coffees rank with the world's best, and Jamaican Blue Mountain, from the Wallensford Estate, is the world's most celebrated (and expensive) coffee. In the summer of 1980, it retailed for around $8 to $12 a pound.

Jamaican Blue Mountain is also one of the most controversial coffees in the world. At this point it is not entirely clear whether any high-quality coffee from the Blue Mountain district of Jamaica is entitled to the name, or whether it properly only applies to coffees grown on a single plantation, the Wallensford Estate. Supposedly only 80 tons of Wallensford Estate Blue Mountain are produced each year, and most of it goes to Japan. Only two

American roasters, Zabar's in New York City and Capricorn Coffees in San Francisco, obtain the Wallensford Estate Blue Mountain directly from the licensed exporter. If you obtain your Blue Mountain from one of these firms or one of the stores they supply, you are drinking the true Wallensford Estate coffee. If you obtain your Blue Mountain from another firm, it may be either Wallensford Blue Mountain which someone has purchased back from Japan, another very similar coffee from the Blue Mountain district but not from the Wallensford Estate, or an ordinary coffee offered at high prices in an attempt to exploit gullible, name-dropping consumers.

Only the taste buds know. If it is true Blue Mountain, and it hasn't staled, it should be absolutely exquisite, the quintessential classic coffee with everything: rich flavor and aroma, full body and moderate acidity in perfect, subtle balance. Whereas Sumatran Mandheling, for instance, is noted above all for its rich, heavy body, Yemen Mocha for its chocolaty tones, Guatemalan Antigua for its smoky tones, and so on, Jamaica Blue Mountain is noted only for its perfection.

A coffee for the rich gourmet who doesn't like extremes. If you prefer a Rolls to a Maserati, buy Jamaican Blue Mountain.

Other coffees from the mountains of Jamaica may be sold as "High Mountain Jamaican" or "Blue Mountain Type Jamaican." These coffees are often excellent, with the smooth balance of true Blue Mountain, but they should be tasted before purchased, and should not cost $8 to $12 a pound.

DOMINICAN REPUBLIC
Santo Domingo

Coffee from the Dominican Republic is often called Santo Domingo, after the country's former name, perhaps because "Santo Domingo" looks so romantic on a coffee bag, and "Dominican Republic" so pedestrian. Coffee is grown on both slopes of the mountain range which runs on an east-west axis down the center of the island. The best grade is simply "washed," and the coffees with the best reputation come from Bani, Ocoa, and Cibao.

Another middle-of-the-road coffee: fair to good body, pleasant but not overbearing acidity.

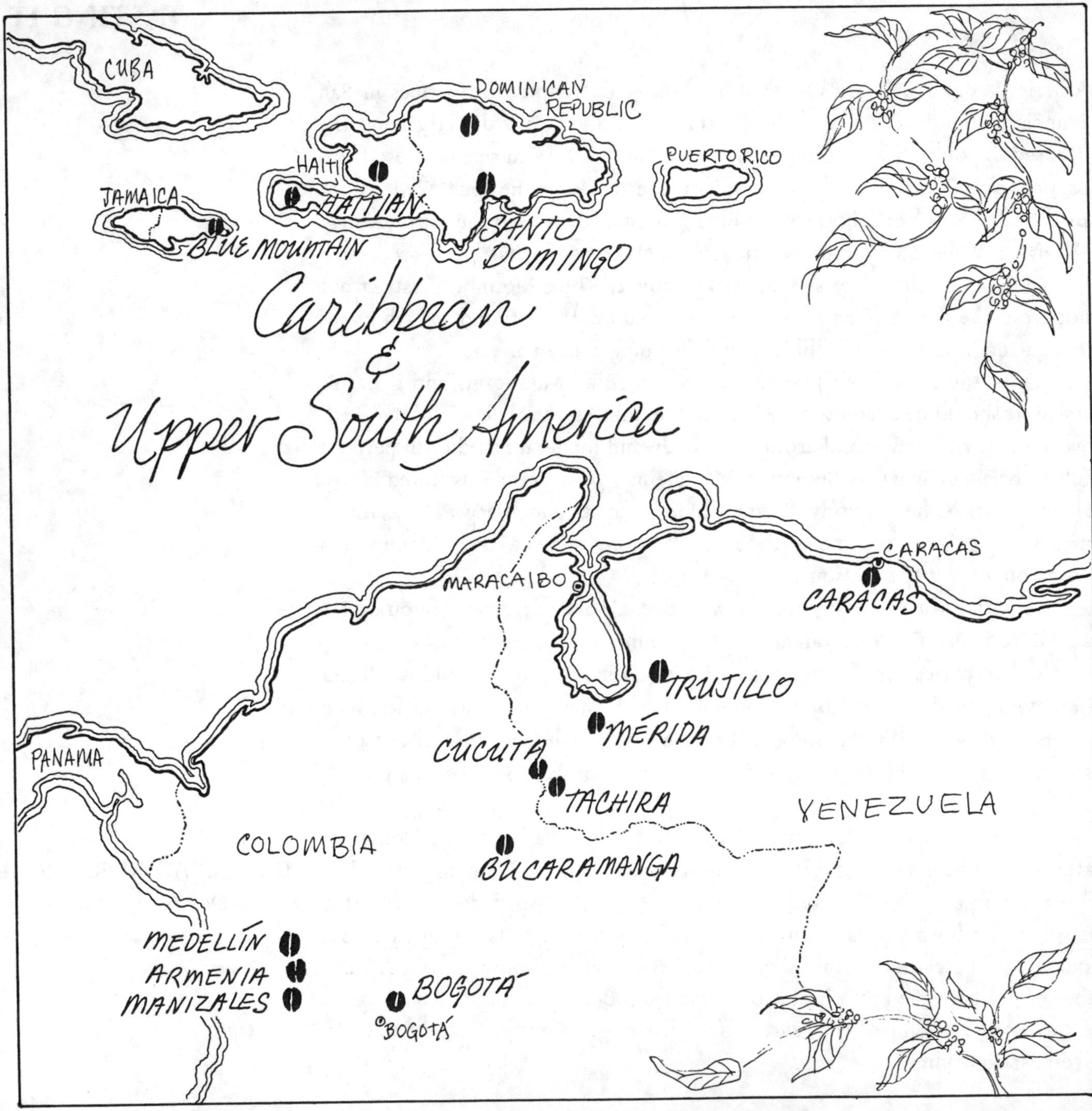

CUBA

DOMINICAN
REPUBLIC

HAITI

PUERTO RICO

JAMAICA

HAITIAN

BLUE MOUNTAIN

*SANTO
DOMINGO*

Caribbean
&
Upper South America

CARACAS

MARACAIBO

CARACAS

TRUJILLO

MÉRIDA

PANAMA

CÚCUTA

TACHIRA

YENEZUELA

COLOMBIA

BUCARAMANGA

MEDELLÍN
ARMENIA
MANIZALES

BOGOTÁ
BOGOTÁ

Haiti, which shares the island of Hispaniola with the Dominican Republic, has a coffee industry built on paradox. On the one hand, most of its coffee is raised on tiny peasant plots and processed by the most primitive of methods. On the other, the Haitian government has promulgated an extraordinarily detailed set of laws and prohibitions apparently intended to upgrade coffee quality by sheer force of edict.

The best of the many grades is "strictly high grown washed"; second best is "high grown washed." The heavy rainfall and deep volcanic soil coupled with the low altitudes may account for the mellow sweetness which distinguishes the best Haitian coffee. It has fair body and acidity to go with the pleasantly soft, rich flavor.

A coffee for sentimental adventurers.

The Colombian coffee industry is the giant of the "mild," or fine, coffee-producing countries of the world. Although it ranks second to Brazil with 12 percent of the world's total coffee production to Brazil's 30 to 35 percent, most of Colombia's 12 percent is great coffee, grown at high altitudes on small peasant holdings, carefully picked, and wet-processed.

Central Colombia is trisected from north to south by three *cordilleras,* or mountain ranges; the central and eastern *cordilleras* produce the best coffees. The principal coffees of the central *cordillera,* going from north to south, are Medellín, Armenia, and Manizales, all named for the towns or cities through which they are marketed. Medellín is the most famous coffee of the three, known for heavy body, rich flavor, and fine, balanced acidity; Manizales and Armenia are in general thinner in body and less acidy. For the purposes of large-scale marketing in the United States, these three coffees are often grouped together as MAMs, an acronym for Medellín-Armenia-Manizales. If your coffee seller is not clear about the precise provenance of his Colombian coffee, it was probably sold as a MAM, which means it could be any of the three.

The two most famous coffees of the eastern *cordillera* are Bogotá, from

Bogotá, Bucaramanga

the region surrounding the capital city of Colombia, and Bucaramanga, marketed through the town of the same name. Bogotá is considered one of Colombia's finest coffees, less acidy than the Medellín, but equally rich and flavorful. The Bucaramanga is a soft-bean coffee, with some of the character of fine Sumatran coffees: heavy body, low acidity, and rich flavor tones.

The highest grade of Colombian is "supremo." But again, to simplify matters for the commercial coffee buyers, the Colombians throw together two grades of coffee, supremo, and the second best, "extra," plus caracol or peaberry of both grades, into one more comprehensive grade, "excelso."

Colombian coffee at its best is like Jamaican Blue Mountain and Costa Rican, a classic. Nothing goes to extreme; it is generally full-bodied, but not so full-bodied as Sumatran, acidy but not nearly as acidy as Ethiopian or Mexican, richly flavored but not quite as rich as Sumatran or Jamaican Blue Mountain. It even has a slight winey tone reminiscent of African coffees, but these winey tones are elusive and never dominate as they do in Ethiopian and some Tanzania.

Another classic coffee, for someone who wants a Rolls but can only afford a BMW.

VENEZUELAN
Maracaibo, Caracas,
Mérida, Cúcuta

At one time, Venezuela ranked close to Colombia in coffee production, but since the discovery and exploitation of petroleum Venezuela seems to have relegated coffee to the economic back burners. Today Venezuela produces less than one percent of the world's coffee, and most of it is drunk by the Venezuelans themselves.

The best Venezuelan coffee comes from the far western corner of the country, the part which nestles up to Colombia. Coffees from this area are called Maracaibos after the port through which they are shipped, and include one coffee, Cúcuta, which is actually grown in Colombia, but shipped through Maracaibo. Coffees from the coastal mountains farther east are generally marked Caracas, after the capital city, and shipped through Caracas' port, La Guaira.

The best-known Maracaibo coffees are Mérida, Trujillo, Tachira, and Cúcuta. Mérida is the most distinctive, and most likely to be found in North American specialty stores. Trujillo is rather lifeless, only a step above the cheap Brazilian coffees. Tachira and Cúcuta are a group in themselves, since their rich acidity makes them resemble Colombian coffees.

The most characteristic Venezuelan coffees, in surprising contrast to the neighbor coffees from Colombia, are strikingly low in acidity. At worst they are spiritless, at best sweet and delicate. The best, like the Méridas, have fair to good body, and an unemphatic but pleasant flavor with hints of richness.

A good coffee to balance sharply acid coffees in blends, and a comfortable coffee drunk straight.

Ecuador, next country south from Colombia along the Andes, produces substantial amounts of coffee, but little seems to appear in North American specialty stores. Another unremarkable coffee, thin to medium body, with occasional sharp acidity.

ECUADOR

Coffee from the Chanchamayo Valley, about 200 miles east of Lima in the high Andes, has the best reputation of the Peruvian coffees, and is more than likely the source for the "Peruvian" at your specialty store. Generally a mildly acid coffee, thin-bodied, but flavorful; resembles the lesser Vera Cruz coffees of Mexico.

PERUVIAN
Chanchamayo

When not suffering catastrophic frosts, Brazil produces something like 30 to 35 percent of the world's coffee. Vast plantations of millions of trees cover the hills of south central Brazil. For the commercial coffee industry Brazil is of supreme importance, a giant in every respect; but for the specialty coffee trade it shrinks to something smaller than El Salvador. For of all the coffee produced in Brazil, none ranks even close to the world's best. The Brazilian coffee industry has concentrated from the beginning on producing "price" coffees: cheap, fairly palatable, but hardly distinguished.

BRAZILIAN
Santos, Bourbon Santos

There are four main coffee-growing regions in Brazil; only one, Santos, is of any importance for the specialty coffee trade; another, "Rio," is significant mainly because it gives its name to a peculiar medicinal flavor which coffee people call "Rioy."

Santos coffees are grown mainly in the state of São Paulo. In the 19th century, Rio coffee's harsh flavor competed in favor with the mild Santos. Much of the famous New Orleans coffee was Rio coffee, with chicory added, and some coffees dark roasted in the United States today for the "Latin taste" may still add Rio coffee to their blend. This is because Latins, who drank the cheap, Rioy-tasting natural coffees at home while the more expensive, washed milds were being sold to the United States, may still crave a bit of the old home-country harshness in their dark-roasted blends, even though they now live on the richer side of the Tropic of Cancer.

Santos coffee, named for one of the principal ports through which it is shipped, comes mainly from the original "Bourbon" strain of *Coffea arabica* brought to Brazil in the 18th century from the island of Bourbon, now Réunion. For the first three or four years these trees produce a small, curly bean which coffee people call "Bourbon Santos." This is the highest-grade coffee Brazil produces, and it will more than likely be the coffee your store sells as "Brazilian." After three or four years the beans begin to grow flat and larger; this coffee is called "flat bean Santos" and is cheaper and less desirable than the Bourbon Santos.

In flavor Bourbon Santos is smooth, in body medium, with moderate acidity; in short, another decent but hardly extraordinary coffee. Since it generally sells for about the same as more distinguished, unusual coffees, I see little reason to buy it except gourmet curiosity. Occasionally one sees the cheaper Brazilian coffees for sale in specialty stores, presumably to be used by the consumer to save money in his private blends.

MOCHA
Yemen, Arabian

"Mocha" is one of the more confusing terms in the coffee lexicon. The coffee we call Mocha today is grown as it has been for hundreds of years in

the mountains of Yemen, at the extreme southwestern tip of the Arabian peninsula. It was originally shipped through the ancient port of Mocha, which has since seen its harbor blocked by a sandbar. But the name Mocha has become so permanently a part of the world's coffee vocabulary that it stubbornly sticks to a coffee which would be more accurately described today as "Yemen" or even "Arabian."

The other ambiguity derives from Arabian Mocha's famed chocolaty aftertaste, which caused some enthusiast to name the traditional mixture of hot chocolate and coffee "mocha." So today "Mocha" is: an old-fashioned nickname for coffee, a common name for coffee from Yemen, Arabia, and the name of a drink made up of coffee and hot chocolate in equal parts.

Aside from the wild coffees of Ethiopia, Arabian Mocha is the most ancient and traditional of coffees, and still one of the best. It is the bean that literally sold the world on coffee. Yemen Mocha is still grown as it was in 600 A.D., on irrigated terraces clinging to the sides of semi-arid mountains; water is directed through little rock-lined channels to the roots of the plants, which are shaded from the desert sun by rows of poplars. The beans are also processed as they have been for centuries; even the best grades (Mocha extra) are "natural" coffees, dried with the fruit still attached to the beans. The dried husk is later removed by millstone or other primitive methods, which accounts for the rough, irregular look of the beans. The names in *Mattari, Sharki,* Yemen coffee are also irregular: No two authorities agree whether they *Sanani* properly indicate grade, district, or variety of bean. But all do agree that Mattari is the best Yemen Mocha, Sharki a close second, and Sanani third.

The plantation coffees of Arabia and Ethiopia, and some Kenya and Tanzania, are the most distinctively flavored coffees in the world. The acidity leaves an unmistakable dry, wine-like aftertaste on the palate. If Mexican coffees can be compared to dry white wines, Mochas and Ethiopians are the Bordeaux of the coffee world. In addition to its rich wininess, Mocha has its own particular flavor note, which some people, with more imagination than accuracy I think, associate with chocolate. Think of

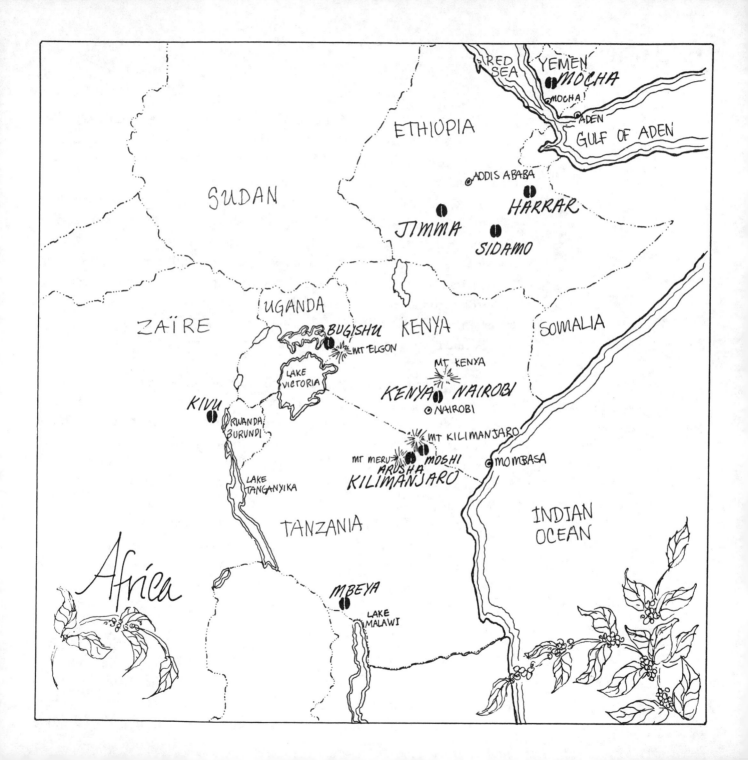

it as chocolate if you like, but don't be disappointed if it doesn't taste like Hershey's. It is a peculiar rich edge to the aftertaste that lurks very clearly but subtly behind the winey acidity. The stronger you make your coffee, the more clearly you will taste the "chocolate" flavor.

Since Mocha is such a distinctive coffee, everyone has something interesting to say about it: "unique," "sharp flavor," "mellow body," "creamy, rich," "distinctive winey flavor," etc. Despite its distinctiveness, I find it a very balanced coffee, with a medium to full body, good but not overwhelming acidity, and a rich flavor with those tantalizing "chocolate" undertones. Its aroma is overwhelming and delicious, heady with tantalizing winey and acidy notes.

A fine coffee. If you think they all taste the same, try this one.

ETHIOPIAN
Harrar, Jimma, Abyssinian

Coffee was first cultivated across the Red Sea in Yemen, but the arabica tree originated on the mountain plateaus of Ethiopia, where tribesmen still harvest the wild berries. The coffee which is usually sold in the United States as "Ethiopian," however, is grown on plantations near the old capital of Harrar or Harari, at about 5,000 to 6,000 feet. You will see it called "Ethiopian Harrar," "longberry Harrar" (large bean), "shortberry Harrar" (smaller bean), or "Mocha Harrar" (peaberry); the "Harrar" may also become "Harari" or "Harar." In Great Britain Harrar is universally sold as "Mocha," adding to the confusion surrounding that abused term.

Ethiopian Harrar is the winiest coffee in the world; you may think someone's spiked your cup with Chianti. The winey quality which some Colombians hint at, which comes through clearly in Mochas, totally triumphs in Ethiopian Harrars. The wininess is strong, gamey, like a rough, dry, light country red wine. Harrar has a light body, however, much lighter than Mocha, and more acidity, which means it lacks Mocha's mellow balance.

A coffee for people who like excitement at the cost of subtlety, those with dull palates, or a craving for the unusual.

The wild coffees of southeastern Ethiopia, which are gathered rather than cultivated, are another matter. They are carelessly picked, processed by the dry method, and are at best bland. You will probably not run across them in your specialty store. They are sold in the trade as "Ethiopian" or "Abyssinian" or by district as "Jimma" or "Djimmah," and "Sidamo."

Although Kenya is only a few hundred miles south of Ethiopia and Yemen, coffee growing came late here. The native Kenyans have taken up what the Germans started and the British perfected, and made the East African coffee industry possibly even more modern and efficient than the Colombian. The coffee is raised both on small peasant plots and on larger plantations.

KENYA
Nairobi

The main growing area stretches south from the slopes of 17,000-foot Mt. Kenya almost to the capital, Nairobi. There is a smaller coffee-growing region on the slopes of Mt. Elgon, on the border between Uganda and Kenya. Most Kenya coffee sold in specialty stores appears to come from the central region around Mt. Kenya, and is sometimes qualified with the name of the capital city, "Nairobi." Grade designates the size of the bean; "AA" is largest, followed, of course, by "A" and "B."

Kenya, like the Arabian Mocha and the Ethiopian Harrar to the north, has a distinctive dry, winey aftertaste. At its best, however, it has a full-bodied richness Ethiopian and even Mocha lacks. A fine coffee for those who like the striking and unusual. Not so winey as the Ethiopian, fuller-bodied, but more intense all around than the Mocha.

Tanzania's coffee industry was at first closely tied to the Kenyan, since early in their national histories they shared common exploiters: first the Germans, then the British. Most Tanzania arabicas are grown on the slopes of Mt. Kilimanjaro and Mt. Meru, near the Kenyan border. These coffees are called "Kilimanjaro," or sometimes "Moshi" or "Arusha" after the main towns and shipping points. Smaller amounts of arabica are grown much farther south, between Lake Tanganyika and Lake Malawi, and are usually

TANZANIA
Kilimanjaro, Moshi

called "Mbeya," after one of the principal towns. In all cases the highest grade is "AA," followed by "A" and "B."

Most Tanzania coffees have the characteristically sharp, winey acidity typical of African and Arabian coffees. They tend to be medium to full-bodied, and fairly rich in flavor. Other arabicas from Tanzania have a totally different character, more akin to the coffees of Sumatra and Celebes: rich, full-bodied, very mellow, and not at all acidy, with hardly a trace of the winey bite of Africa.

An excellent coffee in either case. Something for everyone: a rich, mellow coffee for those who like comfort, and another bright, winey coffee for those who crave the exotic.

UGANDA
Bugishu

The main part of Uganda's production is robusta, used in instant coffees and as cheap fillers in blends. Uganda does produce one excellent arabica, however: Bugishu, from the western slopes of Mt. Elgon, on the Kenyan border. It is another typically winey African coffee, close to the Kenyan coffees in flavor, but lighter in body.

MYSORE
Indian

Mysore is a state in southern India which grows most of India's arabica coffees. Specialty coffee sellers usually call this coffee "Mysore" after the state, rather than "Indian." Legend attributes the first coffee trees in India to a Moslem pilgrim, Baba Budan, who is supposed to have smuggled seven coffee seeds out of Mecca and brought them back to Mysore strapped to his belly around 1600. His seed flourished, but more than likely the Mysore coffee you buy now is from seed introduced later by the British. The best grades are "arabica plantation A and B," and "arabica cherry AB"; the best-known regional names are Baba Budan, Niligris, and Sheverays.

In general, I have found Mysore to be a fairly full-bodied coffee with low acidity, and rather lifeless in flavor and aroma. It strikes me as a coffee which might well mellow out a very acid coffee in a blend, but I wouldn't

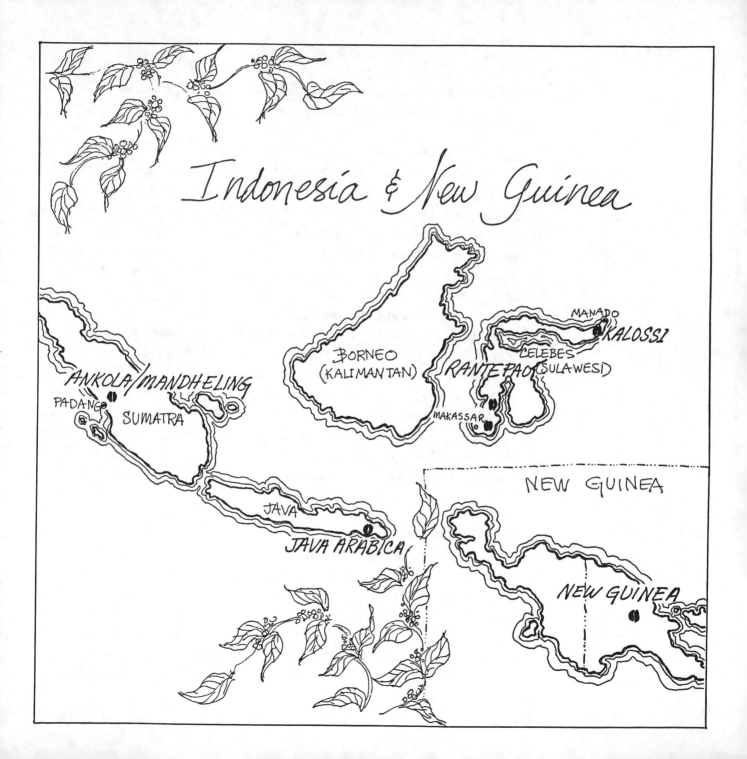

recommend it on its own. Those who like a mellow, low-acid coffee with heavy body would be better buying a Sumatran.

SUMATRAN
Mandheling, Ankola

Some of the most famous coffees of the world are grown on the gigantic islands of the Malay Archipelago: Sumatra, Celebes, and Java in Indonesia, and Papua New Guinea. While Central American coffees are distinguished by their dry, winey aftertaste, the coffees of Indonesia and New Guinea are noted for their richness, full body, and an acidity which, though pronounced, is deep-toned and gentle. They are perfect for those who want a coffee heavy enough to carry its flavor through milk. Indonesian coffees are leisurely. There is something warm and reflective about them; they remind me of gigantic meals and wicker chairs.

Many consider the Mandheling and Ankola coffees of Sumatra the world's finest. They are often hard to find, but still moderate in price. Of the two, Mandheling is the more admired. They are both grown near the port of Padang in west central Sumatra, at altitudes of 2,500 to 5,000 feet. Mandheling is probably the most full-bodied coffee in the world; you can feel the richness settling in the corners behind your tongue. It has a relatively low acidity, but enough to keep the cup vibrant and interesting. The flavor, like the body, is rich, smooth, and full.

A coffee for fulfilled romantics.

CELEBES
Sulawesi, Kalossi,
Rantepao

The island of Sulawesi or Celebes spreads like a four-fingered hand in the middle of the Malay Archipelago. Celebes Kalossi, another of the world's most famous coffees, is grown near the port of Manado, on the southern-most finger. The samples I have tasted make it very similar to Sumatran Mandheling, but possibly a little less rich and full-bodied, and a bit more acidy and vibrant in the upper tones. Coffee from the south of the island, marketed as Rantepao, is excellent, but less admired.

Another gourmet coffee for those who prefer richness and full body to brightness and dry snap.

The Dutch planted the first arabica trees in Java early in coffee history, and before the rust disease virtually wiped out the industry, Java led the world in coffee production. Most of this early acreage has been replaced by disease-resistant robusta, but arabica has made a mild comeback.

JAVA
Java Arabica

Java at its best is another full-bodied, rich coffee. It is perhaps a little more acidy than Sumatran or Celebes, with a slight smoky or spicy twist to the acidity. It is this quality which leads people to call it "pungent," "strong-flavored," or "spicy," though I find these descriptions overstated.

"Old Government," "Old Brown," or simply, "Old" Java describe Java arabica that has been held in warehouses for two to three years. Such "matured" coffee turns from green to light brown, gains body and sweetness, and loses acidity. It was one of the world's great gourmet coffees until it disappeared from the market after World War II. It has recently been revived, although it remains difficult to obtain in the United States. It is readily available in Great Britain, however, and visitors there should take the opportunity to sample it. It is a fine variation on the Indonesian theme: heavy-bodied, rich, and darkly sweet.

Old Java

Coffee labeled "New Guinea" comes from Papua New Guinea, which occupies the eastern half of the island of New Guinea. It is grown in peasant patches and small plantations throughout the rugged mountain highlands. The best New Guinea is estate, or plantation grown.

NEW GUINEA

In general, New Guinea is a low-key version of the great Indonesian coffees: not as full-bodied as the best Sumatran, less acidy and aromatic than the best Celebes, but a comfortably rich cup.

You haven't space-warped your way into the wrong book; there is indeed a *coffee* from China. It is grown in the mountains of Yunnan Province, People's Republic of China, close to the China-Vietnam border. It is furthermore a splendid coffee, for which I predict a great future. Currently it is little known in North America, and less imported. Its presence in

YUNNAN
China

California is owing to Milt Mountanos, whose United Coffee Corporation of San Francisco has created a market for it on the West Coast.

Yunnan resembles the best Indonesian coffees, with hints of Mysore. It has Mysore's low-acid sweetness, but the richness, full body and strong character of Sumatran Mandheling. And lurking subtly but unmistakably in the background is another of those teasing there-it-is, there-it-isn't again flavor notes, analogous to the smokiness of Guatemalan and the chocolate tones of Mocha. In Yunnan it is an evanescent, spicy sweetness, like the scent of sandalwood incense a moment after the smoke has vanished; it is most definitely a *Chinese* flavor.

KONA
Hawaiian

Kona, on the southwest coast of the biggest island of the Hawaiian chain, is the only significant coffee-growing district in Hawaii, although coffee is grown in smaller quantities elsewhere on the islands. In the Kona district, the trees are shaded by a cloud cover that appears like clockwork around two o'clock in the afternoon (the famous "automatic shade"), just in time to protect them from the full devastation of the tropical sun.

But despite the excellence of growing conditions and the fame of the brew, Kona coffee is a disappearing luxury. The Kona industry has always been small—the entire growing area is only two miles wide by 25 miles long—but until recently it boasted the largest production per acre in the world. Today, Kona not only produces less coffee per acre than it did 10 years ago, but the number of acres devoted to coffee has also diminished. The reason: a tourist-inflated economy boosts costs, while world coffee prices, based on low labor costs in other tropical countries, remain relatively low. Most Kona coffee is grown on small five- to seven-acre farms by Japanese and Portuguese farmers who in 1975 averaged 68 years old. The 1977 price hikes helped stimulate the industry, and abandoned coffee farms began to be reclaimed and put back into production. If this revival lasts, we can continue to enjoy an excellent coffee, not one of the world's great coffees perhaps, but worthy of appreciation, and certainly preservation.

Kona coffee is medium-bodied, fairly acidy, with some subtle winey tones, very richly flavored, and overwhelmingly aromatic. If you like to tantalize yourself with odor before you drink, or find Indonesian coffees too rich, African coffees too winey, and those of Central and South America too sharp, Kona may be the coffee for you.

MARAGOGIPE

Maragogipe is a variety of arabica, which produces a very large, rather porous bean. It is a mutant spontaneously produced in Brazil, almost as though the Sleeping Giant of the Americas thought regular beans were too puny and produced something in its own image. It was first discovered growing near the town of Maragogipe, in the southeastern state of Bahia. Subsequently it has been carried all over the world, and generally adopts the flavor characteristics of the soil to which it has been transplanted.

Opinions differ about the special qualities of the Maragogipe. William H. Ukers, one of the world's great authorities on coffee, found it tasted "woody and disagreeable" in 1928. Others have called it "the finest coffee known," and claim it will have a heavier body than a comparable arabica coffee from the same region. I've compared a Guatemalan Maragogipe with other Guatemalan arabicas and found it less acidy, lighter in body, and flatter in flavor. This last test is hardly conclusive, however, since the Maragogipe I tried may have come from lower altitudes than the arabicas. Like any other straight coffee, Maragogipes should be sold by country of origin.

PEABERRY

Peaberry, or caracol, is a grade of coffee, rather than a botanical variety. All over the world the coffee fruit occasionally produces a single, rather than double, bean. This loner grows to be small and round, with a tiny crevice splitting it halfway down the middle.

Coffee folklore has it that peaberry grades are superior to normal grades from the same crop, apparently on the basis that the good stuff that ordinarily goes into two beans goes into only one bean in the case of the peaberry. If anything, however, coffee from peaberries tends to be lighter in body and flavor than coffee from high-grade normal beans from the same trees.

Peaberry coffee should be sold by country and market name like any other coffee. If you see a sign that simply says "Peaberry," you should inquire as to the coffee's origin.

AGED COFFEES

As it ages green coffee loses acidity and, depending on how it is stored, gains body. Coffee delivered for roasting soon after harvest and processing is called "new crop." Coffee which has been held in warehouses for a period before delivery is called "old crop." "Mature" coffees are usually two to three years old. Aged or "vintage" coffees, which have been held in dry and well-ventilated warehouses for six to 10 years, constitute a fourth category. Under these conditions the acidity disappears entirely and is replaced by a peculiar syrupy richness. In general, coffees with full body and robust flavor age better than the more delicate growths.

At present few aged coffees are available; aging coffees represents a long-term capital investment most contemporary exporters are unwilling to take. One occasionally sees aged Venezuelan and Colombian coffees for sale in specialty stores, however, and aged Sumatran and Celebes are available, but seldom sold as straight coffees. You ought to try an aged coffee at least once; you will immediately note a rather dull, sweet heaviness, not at all like the more stimulating richness of a full-bodied new crop coffee or the still-lively sweetness of a "mature" coffee.

If you are anti-acidity to the point of fanaticism, you might like a straight aged coffee. They are most useful, however, in blends to give body and sweetness to "young," dry, sharply acid coffees.

BLENDING YOUR OWN

Since blending is the ultimate proof of coffee expertise, and since it gives the consumer a chance unusual in today's marketplace to participate in the creation of his own pleasure, specialty coffee customers often take to blending their own coffees. The only drawback to such a pleasant practice is impatience: The consumer may decide to begin blending before he knows enough to do it right, and the seller may get frustrated if he has to stop to make a blend of five coffees for a customer when there are 10 more customers waiting in line behind him. But let's let the seller take care of himself. Few storekeepers will object if they feel the customer is really blending, rather than just showing off or demanding attention, and it's your money anyhow.

One can blend different roasts, coffees with different caffeine contents, or straight coffees from different countries. One of the more common practices is to blend dark and light roasts, a procedure I discuss in detail in Chapter 2. Another reason to blend is to cut caffeine content. If you drink only decaffeinated coffee you may get bored, since specialty shops carry at most two caffeine-free coffees. If you drink only straight coffee you may get insomnia. An excellent compromise is to blend a caffeine-free coffee with your favorite straight coffees, thus cutting your caffeine intake while maintaining your spirit of adventure.

blending roasts

The art of blending straight coffees of the same roast is a subtler business, but hardly difficult once the basic principles are understood. Blenders who work for large commercial coffee companies need to be highly skilled because their job is more complex than ours. All we want to do is blend a coffee that suits us better than a single straight coffee would, taken alone. But the commercial blender also blends to cut costs while keeping quality up, and wants to assemble a blend that always tastes the same even though the straight coffees that make up the blend may differ. Certain coffees are not available at all times, some coffees may be cheaper than others at certain times of the year, and so on. But in an economy dominated by highly advertised brand names the blend has to taste more or less the same every time. So the blender may at times find himself tap dancing at the center of a shifting kaleidoscope of prices and availabilities, constantly juggling coffees in an attempt to keep the taste the same and the cost down.

blending straight coffees

A good commercial blend takes a fresh, sharp, acidy, aromatic coffee like Colombian, Costa Rican, or Mexican, and combines it with a decent grade of Brazilian coffee to cut costs. If it's a very high-priced blend, the blender might combine more than one quality coffee with the Brazilian: a rich, full-bodied coffee to balance a bright, acidy coffee for instance. Low-cost blends might decrease the proportion of mild coffee and Brazilian, and make up the difference with a very bland and inexpensive robusta. The very cheapest blends eliminate the high-priced mild coffee entirely, and simply combine a decent grade of Brazilian with the robustas.

Specialty coffee roasters usually have their own blends. A small roaster may have only one, his "house blend," or he may have as many as a half-dozen for all pocketbooks, tastes, and times of day.

less to consider

The consumer who makes his own blends has less to consider than the commercial blender. He shouldn't have to worry about consistency, and he can't use blending to bring the price down much, since most straight coffees sold through specialty stores are already premium coffees with premium prices. It would be like trying to save money by cutting caviar with truffles, or mixing 110 octane gas with 100 octane gas. Commercial coffee concerns can save money on their blends because they are able to buy large quantities of cheap coffee at bargain prices. As I indicated in Chapter 4, a more effective way to save money would be to buy green coffee in bulk and learn to roast it yourself.

principle of blending

So all you will be blending for is taste. The way to go about this is simple: You combine coffees which complement one another with qualities the others lack. The world's oldest and most famous blend, for instance, combines Arabian Mocha and Java. Part of the reason for its fame is of course tradition: It began when Mocha and Java were the only coffees available. Nevertheless, it embodies the sound principle of balancing extremes, or complements. Remember that Mocha is a mildly acidy, winey coffee with a fairly light body; Java is a heavier-bodied coffee, sweeter and deeper-toned. Put together they make a brew which is both less and more—less striking and distinctive, but more balanced and comprehensive.

Your first, and pleasurable, task in assembling a personal blend is to learn to distinguish acidity, body, and flavor in coffee, and possibly some of the more individual quirks: the dry aftertaste of African coffees, the smoky tones of Guatemalan Antigua. By then you should also know what qualities you prefer in a coffee, and what to blend for. You may simply want an all-around coffee, with the best of all worlds, or you may want a basically heavy, mellow coffee with only a little acidy brightness, or a brisk, light coffee with plenty of body, too.

But always proceed the same way. If you have a favorite coffee which seems to lack something, combine it with a coffee that has in extreme form what your favorite lacks:

recommendations

- For brightness, snap, acidity, add Costa Rican, Colombian, Guatemalan, or any of the good Central American coffees.
- For body and richness, add Sumatran Mandheling, Celebes Kalossi, or Java.
- For sweetness, add Venezuelan Maracaibo or Haitian.
- For even more sweetness, or to dull a bright coffee, add an aged coffee or a Mysore.
- For flavor and aroma, add Kona, Jamaican Blue Mountain, Sumatran, Celebes, Guatemalan, or Colombian.
- To add a winey note, make the acidy coffee an Ethiopian; to add richness as well, make it a Kenya or Mocha.

The only real mistake one can make in blending is to combine two coffees which are distinctive or extreme in the same way. Two coffees with sharp, winey acidity like a Kenya and an Ethiopian, for example, would make a poor blend. Better combine an Ethiopian with a richer, low-key coffee like a Mysore. One has to be particularly beware of the distinctive, gamey coffees of Africa, which may make a dissonant blend with other acidy coffees. On the other hand, some coffees like Mysore or most Venezuelans, are so congenially understated that they get along with everybody. Others,

blending friends and enemies

like Mocha and the large Latin American family of coffees, are easy-going individualists who manage to get along with almost everybody, yet still maintain their distinction.

Dark-roasted coffee is sometimes blended with chicory, particularly in northern France and the southern United States. Chicory is an easily grown, disease-resistant relative of the dandelion. The young leaves, when used for salad, are called endive. The root resembles the dandelion root, and when dried, roasted, and ground, produces a deeply brown, full-bodied, almost syrupy beverage which has a bitter peppery tang, and doesn't taste at all like coffee. In fact, it tastes like someone put some pepper in your herbal tea mixture. It is almost impossible to drink black; sweetened with milk it makes a fairly satisfying hot beverage, though it leaves a bitter, cloying aftertaste.

first use

According to Heinrick Jacob in *Coffee: The Epic of a Commodity*, some Germans first exploited the use of chicory as a coffee substitute around 1770. The Germans, who are probably more suspicious of the skeptical, sober, Apollonian effects of caffeine than any other nation, adopted chicory because it had no caffeine and (possibly most important) because it eluded the tariffs imposed on foreign luxuries like coffee. Jacob describes the trademark on 18th century packets of chicory: "A German farmer sowing chicory seed, and waving away ships freighted with coffee beans. Beneath was the legend: 'Without you, Healthy and rich.'"

But it was under Napoleon's "continental system," a sort of reverse blockade aimed at cutting England off from its European markets and making conquered Europe self-sufficient, that chicory came into its own. The French developed the sugar beet to replace sugarcane, but the chicory root was the best they could come up with for coffee. Not much of a substitute, since it has neither caffeine nor coffee's aromatic oils. After the collapse of the Napoleonic empire, the French went back to coffee, but never totally lost their taste for chicory.

The famous New Orleans-style coffee, which came to the southern United States with the French colonists, tastes the way it does for three reasons: it has chicory in it, the beans are dark roasted, and some cheap, naturally processed Brazilian beans are added to give the brew that old-time sour twist. If you like New Orleans-style coffee and want to carry your taste to more refined levels, you need to first determine which components account for what you like about the flavor: the chicory, the dark roast, or the sour beans.

New Orleans coffee

I assume by now you've tried dark-roast coffee. Next, buy ground French chicory, sold at most large specialty coffee stores. It costs a little less than coffee, and goes farther, which is another reason for developing a taste for New Orleans-style coffee. Now simply experiment by varying the proportions of chicory to ground dark-roast coffee. About 10 percent chicory will barely effect flavor, but will considerably increase the body and darkness of the brew. You get the peppery taste clearly at 20 percent, but it still doesn't overpower the coffee flavor, and you can drink such a blend black with pleasure. Most New Orleans blends are 30 to 40 percent chicory. At these proportions the bitter chicory flavor at least equals the coffee flavor, and I think most people would have trouble drinking such a blend black.

percentages

If you mix chicory and dark-roast coffee and it still doesn't taste as good to you as the canned commercial New Orleans blends, then it's the cheap natural beans you like, and you probably can't buy them unless you find a Latin American roaster who will let you have some green.

In Great Britain, a blend of coffee and roast ground fig is popular. Fig has a flavor very different from the heavy, peppery bite of chicory. Mixed in proportions of one part fig to seven parts ground coffee, fig adds considerable body and a delicate, fruity sweetness to the cup. I much prefer it to chicory, but since it's unavailable commercially in the United States and most readers will hardly bother to roast and grind it themselves, I won't carry on about it.

4 ROASTING IT
How coffee is roasted and how to roast your own

SINCE WE HAVE COME to associate the word coffee so absolutely with a hot, aromatic brown liquid, some may find it hard to believe that mankind had to fuss for several hundred years before concluding that the most interesting way to get what it wanted from the coffee tree was to roast the dried kernel of the fruit, grind it, and toss the resulting powder into hot water. The alternative solutions are many, and some still survive as part of the cuisine of Africa and Asia. The berries can be fermented to make a wine, for example, or the leaves and flowers cured and steeped in boiling water, to produce a coffee tea. In parts of Africa people soak the raw beans in water and spices, and chew them like candy. The raw berries are also combined with bananas, crushed, and beaten to make a sort of raw coffee and banana smoothie.

The key to the victory of the current mode of coffee making is the roasting process, to which we owe the delicately flavored oils that speak to the palate as eloquently as caffeine to the sleep-numbed nervous system. "The coffee berries are to be bought at any Druggist," says a 17th century English pamphlet on coffee drinking, "about three shillings a pound; take what quantity you please and over a charcoal fire, in an old pudding pan or

delicate oils

69

ROASTING IT

frying pan, keep them always stirring til they be quite black, and yet if you exceed, they do you waste the Oyl, which only makes the drink; and if less, they will it not deliver its Oyl, which must make the drink."

We may not agree with the Englishman's taste in roasting ("quite black" sounds more Neapolitan than English), but he knew what counted: The breaking down of fats and carbohydrates into an aromatic, volatile, oily substance which alone produces coffee flavor and aroma. Without roasting, the bean will give up its caffeine, acids, even its protein, but not its flavor.

chemistry The chemistry of coffee roasting is complex, and still not completely understood. This is owing to the variety of beans, as well as the complexity of the coffee essence, which is kinky enough to still defy chemists' best efforts to duplicate it in the laboratory.

Much of what happens to the bean in roasting is interesting, but irrelevant: The bean loses a lot of moisture, for instance, which means it weighs less after roasting than before (a fact much lamented among penny-conscious commerical roasters). It loses some protein, about 10 to 15 percent of its caffeine, and traces of other chemicals. Sugars are burned or caramelized, which contributes color and some body to the cup.

simple in theory Roasting is simple in theory: The beans must be heated, kept moving so they don't burn or roast unevenly, and cooled (or "quenched") when the right moment has come to stop the roasting. Coffee which is not roasted long enough or hot enough to bring out the oil will have a pasty, nutty, or bread-like flavor. Coffee which is roasted too long or at too high a temperature will be thin-bodied, burned, and industrial-flavored; very badly burned coffee will taste like old sneakers left on the radiator. Coffee roasted too long at too low a temperature will have a baked flavor.

Most roasting equipment uses a rotating drum with a heat source under it, usually a gas flame. The whole effect is a lot like a laundromat clothes drier. The rotating drum tumbles the beans, assuring an even roast. The air temperature inside the drum is usually controlled at about 500°F; for the first five minutes, the bean merely loses "free" moisture, moisture which is not bound up in the cellular structure of the bean. Eventually, however, the deep "bound" moisture begins to force its way out, expanding the bean and producing a snapping or crackling noise. So far, the color of the bean has not appreciably changed (it should be a light brown), and the oil has not been volatilized. Then, when the interior temperature of the bean reaches about 400°F, the oil quite suddenly begins developing; chemists call this process pyrolysis; it is marked visually by a darkening in the color of the bean.

pyrolysis

This is the moment of truth for the coffee roaster, machine or human, because the pyrolysis, or volatilization of the coffee essence, must be stopped at precisely the right instant to obtain the flavor and roast desired. The beans cannot be allowed to cool of their own accord, or they may over-roast. They are quickly dumped into a metal box, where pyrolysis continues until "quenched" with either cold air or a light spray of cold water. Most specialty roasters air-quench their coffee.

The exact nature of the roasting equipment depends on the ambitions of the roaster. Let's start with a big-time commercial roaster, work our way down through a small, store-front roaster, and from there to you and me in our kitchens. The coffee bean, when delivered to the roaster in big burlap sacks, ranges in color from light brown to whitish green. The beans are always stored green; roasted whole beans begin to deteriorate in flavor within a week after roasting, and ground coffee may taste stale within an hour after grinding, whereas green coffee may even improve with age.

equipment

The large commercial roaster resembles a big screw rotating inside a drum; the screw works the coffee down the drum. By the time the coffee reaches the end of the drum it is roasted, and ready to be cooled by air or water. The temperature is controlled automatically, and there may even be equipment that monitors the temperature inside the beans, to assure uniform roast. Such roasters are called "continuous" roasters for obvious reasons and are inappropriate for specialty roasters for several reasons: they cost too much, roast too much at a time, don't permit direct control of the roasting process, and don't work very well for dark roasts.

commercial roasters

ROASTING IT

The average specialty roaster uses a "batch" roaster, which is simply a rotating drum with heat under it; when the coffee is ready the roaster dumps the "batch" of coffee into a metal box where it is cooled. These batch roasters may be as large around as four or five feet, or as small as a small trash can set on its side.

On the facing page you'll find a picture of a typical small batch roaster. The drum (A) tumbles the roasting coffee over the gas flame (B). The fan (C) sucks the smoke and chaff out of the drum. When the beans are dumped into the cooling box (D) and ready to be quenched, the fan is reversed, and cool air is forced back through the hot beans at D.

Roasters, like cooks and artists, tend to fall into two schools: those who depend on an abstract system and those who follow their eyes, ears, nose and intuition. A systematic roaster might roast all his coffees for the same period of time, for instance, but roast each at a different temperature depending on the color of roast he wants plus the bean's hardness, or resistance to heat. These temperatures, based on tests, would all be a matter of written record. Thus the roasting process in theory could be duplicated by anyone who could read and set dials.

an intuitive roaster

For an example of an intuitive roaster, let me introduce the memory of the Graffeo coffee shop in San Francisco, locally famous for its rich, sweet espresso coffee. At that time the roasting was done in a small, old-fashioned batch roaster by John Repetto, the father of the present proprietor, and an intuitive roaster if there ever was one.

Three open bags of green coffee stood next to the roasting machine. Two contained coffees from South and Central America, one with lighter and one with heavier body; in the third bag was a mix of four or five sharp, distinctively flavored coffees: Arabian Mocha, Kenya, or Ethiopian, for instance. With a fine nonchalance, Mr. Repetto would scoop about equal parts of each into the rotating drum of the roasting machine, close the door, and turn up the flame. Thereafter he wandered around the store, waiting on

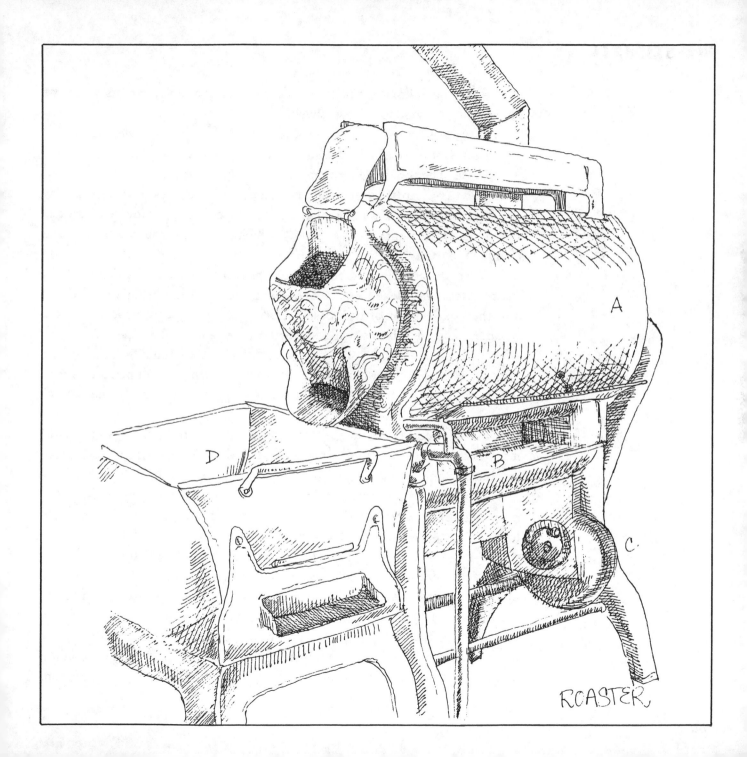

customers and following this timetable, which anyone who roasts coffee at home would be wise to follow as well:

One: Coffee smells like the sack (do something else for a while).

Two: Coffee smells like bread (do it closer to the roaster).

Three: The beans begin to crackle (prepare for action).

When he heard them crackle, Mr. Repetto knew the oil was developing and began checking the color of the beans by collecting a few with a little spoon-like implement called a "trier," which is stuck through a hole in the front of the roasting cylinder.

When the color was about medium brown (the shop sells mainly dark-roast coffee), he opened a door in the cylinder, and the beans tumbled out into the box in front of the roaster. Here the roasting continued inside the steaming, crackling beans while he stirred them and studied them for color. When they were dark brown ("the color of a monk's tunic"), he tripped a lever on the side of the fan box, forcing cold air up through perforations at the bottom of the box to stop the roasting process at exactly the correct moment.

"the color of a monk's tunic"

Much specialty coffee is roasted in similar fashion in similar old machines, some large, some small, most with a loveable early industrial-revolution look. Other specialty roasting firms, as I indicated, work on a much larger scale with more up-to-date equipment. I recall my disappointment when I revisited the Graffeo shop and found the old roasting machine holding up plants in the store window and John's son, Luciano, wearing a white smock and watching some dials on the front of a chrome box. This box I recognized as a Sivitz roaster, the creation of Michael Sivitz, a well-known technical writer on coffee who some years before had gone into the business of producing his own coffee roasting equipment based on a new principle. Rather than rotating the beans inside a cylinder, the Sivitz machine suspends the beans in a floating mass atop a rapidly moving column of hot air. Mr. Sivitz claims that his system, which prevents the beans from

ARABIAN COFFEE ROASTING

ROASTING IT

touching hot metal for longer than a moment, produces a more uniform roast than the traditional drum roaster.

Perhaps. The coffee tastes good from the new machine, and it tasted good from the old. One thing is certain: Buying from the person who roasts the coffee is your best assurance of a fresh coffee, and a good coffee.

ROASTING YOUR OWN

Those who want to be absolutely certain their coffee is fresh—in fact, anyone who wishes to drink the absolutely best cup of coffee possible—should experiment with roasting their own coffee at home. Home roasting is very simple, and very quick. It takes about as much time and skill as cooking spaghetti, and is considerably simpler than other more fashionable back-to-basics activities, like baking your own bread or making your own beer. And any small mistakes in the roasting process are far offset by the advantages of freshness.

Roasted, ground coffee is in the larger perspective as much a convenience food as instant coffee or frozen foods. Americans roasted their own coffee until late into the nineteenth century, and many people all over the world still do. Jabez Burns, inventor of the continuous roaster, the first modern production roaster, insisted that some of the best roasted coffee he ever tasted was done in a corn popper.

The physical requirements for roasting coffee correctly are very simple: the coffee needs to be kept moving in air temperatures of at least 400°F, and to be cooled at the correct moment.

isolated individualists

People who roast coffee at home, being the isolated individualists they are, unconfirmed in their activity by newspaper articles or TV commercials, are usually convinced that their way is the only way. There are two basic schools, however: the top-of-the-stove, shake-'em approach, and the in-the-oven, iron-skillet school. In the interests of forestalling conflict and reducing roasting-method chauvinism, I offer instructions below for both approaches.

For the top-of-the-stove method, you need the following: a lightweight aluminum pan with a metal handle and a fairly tightfitting cover; a sturdy oven thermometer which will fit inside the covered pan; a nose, ears and eyes; and a sample bean from the shop already roasted to your taste. And of course you need the green coffee, which can usually be purchased from any shop that roasts its own. Remember, beans swell when they're roasted, so don't be shocked if your package looks small. The pan should have a metal handle, since a plastic handle may start to burn when the pan is heated empty at high temperatures. The pan I use is the bottom part of an aluminum egg poacher I bought at a supermarket. I've been roasting coffee in it for years, and it shows no signs of fatigue.

Put the thermometer in the pan, put the pan on the flame, and cover. Most inexpensive oven thermometers have a flat piece of metal projecting from the lower back of the thermometer so you can stand the thermometer upright on the floor of your oven. This metal projection will now serve to keep the body of the thermometer off the bottom of the pan. If your thermometer doesn't have such a metal projection, you may have to buy one that does, since it would be unwise to place the body of the thermometer, the part that registers heat, directly on the bottom surface of the pan. It would then register the temperature of the metal at the bottom of the pan, rather than the temperature of the *air inside the pan,* which is your intention.

air temperature

Start with a low heat and raise it until the temperature inside the pan steadies at around 500°F. Make sure you have your sample bean handy. Next, toss in enough green beans to cover the bottom of the pan to a depth of half an inch or so, and *cover again immediately.* In general, you want to lift the cover as little as possible, so as to maintain a high, even temperature inside the pan.

If the temperature inside the pan decreases to below 400°F, turn up the heat. Now, holding the cover, begin gently shaking the beans. You should continue shaking them at one-minute intervals until the roasting is over. The shaking is important, because the surface of the pan is so hot that the beans will roast unevenly if they're allowed to rest for long. Peek in at the thermometer occasionally to make sure the temperature is holding at 400°F.

beans will crackle

Soon the beans will begin to crackle, and a pungent smoke will start seeping out around the cover. This indicates pyrolysis has started. Keep shaking for about a minute or so longer, then lift the cover and peer inside at the beans. When the average color is a little lighter than your sample bean, remove the pan from the heat, take off the cover, and shake or stir the beans until they reach the exact color of your sample. At this point dump them into a second bowl or pan. When they have cooled, store them in an airtight jar just as you would any whole-bean coffee.

After a few tries you should be able to dispense with the thermometer, since you'll have enough experience to adjust the heat and timing freehand. Again, there is no need to be overly fastidious about the process. If your roast is slightly scorched or more darkly roasted in some places than others, don't be alarmed. It should still taste fine. Badly scorched beans will ruin flavor, however.

corn poppers

Stove-top corn poppers that closely resemble 19th-century home coffee roasters are available in many specialty coffee stores. These essentially are covered pans with a crank on top that rotates two vanes inside the pan. Instead of shaking the beans you turn the crank, shoving the beans around inside the pan. These old-timey looking items retail anywhere from $10 to $20. If you buy one, try it out first in the store with some green beans to make sure the fit between the vanes and the bottom of the pan is snug. In some that I've tried the beans hang up between the vanes and the bottom, making the crank hard to turn.

If you do use a cranking corn popper you'll have to use your oven thermometer first to establish the proper temperature before you start pushing the beans around, then remove it to prevent it getting in the way.

For the in-the-oven, iron-skillet method, spread about half an inch or so *iron-skillet* of the green beans in an iron frying pan and place the pan in an oven *method* preheated to 500°F. The difficult part of this method is the need to open the oven every one or two minutes and give the beans a stir with a spatula. In other respects, follow the instructions given above. Remember to remove the pan from the oven when the moment for cooling nears, so you can study the beans closely for correct color.

A last method of home roasting deserves mention: Michael Sivitz, the coffee-roaster pioneer mentioned earlier, has developed a home roaster based on his principle of suspending roasting beans atop a column of rapidly moving heated air. This mini-Sivitz roaster is fun but impractical. If you choose to roast more than an ounce of beans at a time you have to shake the contraption anyhow, and regardless of how little you roast, chaff from the beans gets blown around the kitchen. But someone with a strong kitchen fan and a soft spot for odd-ball technology might want to order one of these gadgets from Mr. Sivitz: $100 postpaid (Michael Sivitz, 3635 N.W. Elmwood Drive, Corvallis, Oregon 97330).

An environmental note: Although only the Sivitz roaster blows chaff around, all home roasting methods produce a heavy, pungent smoke that is pleasant smelling at first, but will make your kitchen stink for days afterwards if you don't ventilate while roasting.

For communes, country families, and similar isolated, back-to-nature types who haven't gone completely herbal, home roasting is ideal. Certainly it would suit exiled epicures who live far from a specialty coffee store. You can get an excellent price on a big sack of green coffee beans, drink much better coffee than most city folks, and cut down on cans, waste and expense.

5 GRINDING IT
Choosing a grind and a grinder

EVERY STEP of the transformation of green coffee into hot brewed coffee makes the flavor essence of the bean more vulnerable to destruction. Green coffees keep for years, with only a slow, subtle change in flavor. But roasted coffees begin to lose their flavor after a week, ground coffee an hour after grinding, and brewed coffee in mere minutes.

The Arabs still have the best solution: roast, grind, brew, and drink the coffee on the spot, all in the same sitting. The whole process takes about half an hour, however, so we'll assume you prefer letting someone else do the roasting. Roasted, whole-bean coffee keeps fairly well. The bean itself is a protective package, albeit a fragile one. Stored in a dry, airtight container to prevent contamination or contact with moisture, roasted whole-bean coffee will keep its flavor and aroma almost perfectly for about a week. After two, it will still taste reasonably fresh, but the aroma will begin slipping; after three the flavor begins to go, and whole-bean coffee kept past a month, while still drinkable, will strike the palate as lifeless and dead.

how long

But if the natural packaging of the bean is broken, in other words if the coffee is ground, it will go stale in a few hours. The delicate oils are exposed and immediately begin evaporating. An airtight container will help, but not

81

much. The oxygen and moisture are in there with the broken coffee, destroying the delicate oils, even if you never open the package again.

a useless gesture

Canning coffee is one of those useless gestures typical of convenience foods. Essentially the natural coffee package, the bean, is broken down, and replaced with a can, an inefficient artificial package. Furthermore, canned coffee is not only pre-ground, but *pre-staled*. Freshly roasted and ground coffee releases carbon dioxide gas. If the coffee were put in the cans fresh, the gas could swell the strongest can and turn it into an egg-shaped time bomb. Various technological solutions have been found to this problem, but none strikes me as in any way conducive to richly flavored coffee. And when the consumer does break open the artificial package, he may find a coffee still relatively fresh—but not for long. Since the thousands of small natural packages that make up a pound of coffee have already been broken into, the oxygen that enters the can every time you peel off the plastic lid rapidly completes the job the canning process started.

grind your own

So the easiest and most effective approach is to break down the bean as close as possible to the moment you want to use it; in other words, *grind your coffee just before you brew it*. Grinding your coffee fresh takes very little time. Grinders are inexpensive, and range from quickie electrics to magnificent replicas of old hand grinders. And there is *no one thing that you can do that will increase the quality of your coffee more*.

ideal routine

So the ideal coffee routine for the urban home would be: Buy the coffee whole bean, preferably a half-pound at a time and preferably from a store where they roast it on the spot. Put it in an airtight container in a cool, dark place, and take out only as much as you want to grind and brew immediately. When I say airtight I mean it. No recycled coffee cans or cottage cheese cartons with snap-on plastic lids; rather a solid glass jar with a rubber gasket inside the cap that gives a good seal, like a mason or old mayonnaise jar.

If buying the coffee in half-pound lots isn't practical because you live in the country, then the airtight container and the grinder become even more important. If you do order your coffee by mail and you know about how much coffee you consume by month, you can put in a standing order with a coffee roaster (see pages 184-185), so your coffee comes fresh every other week, a couple of pounds at a time.

Freezing whole beans isn't a bad idea, providing they're tightly wrapped and you don't refreeze them. Some suppliers recommend that you keep even your day-to-day supply of whole beans in the freezer, and take out only as many as you wish to consume at a time. But freezing coffee is still an expedient. Even frozen, the oil seems to lose flavor and aroma. How about selling your home and moving next door to a coffee roaster?

Some people recommend refrigerating coffee, but I'm against it. Refrigerators are both damp and smelly, and moisture and odors are archenemies of fresh coffee. Even if you keep the coffee in an airtight jar, the changes in temperature every time you take the jar out of the refrigerator will help destroy freshness. Stick to freezing for long-term storage, and an airtight jar in a cool dark place for short-term.

There is an awesome number of grinders on the market. There is even a lot of *kinds* of grinders. So before I launch into my techno-historico-cultural analysis of grinders presently available, I'd like to offer some "first choice" recommendations.

BUYING A GRINDER

For anyone who has half a muscle, loves coffee, and has a large kitchen, I suggest the Quaker City "OB" grain grinder, available at a few coffee specialty stores for $20 to $25, or for less through the manufacturer (Nelson & Sons, Inc., P.O. Box 1296, Salt Lake City, Utah 84110). It's cheap, and so far as I can tell, there is no better grinder available at any price. It will grind coffee as fine as the finest Middle Eastern or "Turkish" style demands; it's fast; the grind is always uniform; the handle is long enough to turn easily; and like all hand grinders, it grinds coffee "cool" (some electric grinders with small, rapidly turning burrs tend to heat the grinding coffee through friction, which "cooks" the essential oils).

first choice

GRINDING IT

Its drawbacks are its looks (like your grandmother's meat grinder); the fact that it needs a table or shelf to clamp onto, which makes it space-consuming; and the fact that it doesn't have a built-in receptacle to catch the ground coffee, which makes it messy. The Spong grinder gets around some of these disadvantages, and at least comes close to the all-around superiority of the Quaker City mill.

Despite the pretentions of modern technology, there are still only four *four ways to grind* ways to grind coffee. The oldest is the mortar and pestle. The next oldest is the millstone, updated to steel burrs or corrugated plates. The next most recent is the roller mill, which is used only in giant commercial grinders. The most recent is the electric blade grinder, which works on the same principle as the electric blender.

If you're *really* into getting back to basics, the mortar and pestle may be the grinder for you. It's cheap, esthetically satisfying, builds up your wrist *mortar and pestle* muscles, and satisfies the profound suspicion so many of us harbor that if it doesn't tire you out it's not really good for you. However, the mortar and pestle does have technical drawbacks: It takes too long, you can't grind much at a time, and it's hard to get an even grind. The price is right, though ($3 to $25).

Which brings us up through history to the next method, and still the best: Very early in its history coffee was ground between the same millstones that the early peoples of the Middle East used to reduce grains to flour. Later, the Turkish-style coffee grinder was evolved, a small cylinder-shaped implement with a crank on the top that looks and works like a pepper mill. Once the big stones became little corrugated steel plates, this sort *millstone* of grinder has actually never been improved upon. All sorts of variations have been developed over the years, including hitching the plates to an electric motor, but the principle remains the same. The heart of the grinder is two little corrugated steel disks, or a corrugated steel cone that fits inside a second hollow corrugated cone. One element is stationary and the other is rotated by a handle or motor. The coffee is fed, a bean or two at a time,

Box grinder

GRINDING IT

between the corrugated disks, where it is crushed until it drops out of the bottom of the grinder. This solution has never been beaten because, one, the *grind is uniform,* and two, by adjusting the space between the plates one can regulate the fineness of the grind accurately and consistently.

box grinders

The cheapest hand grinders are the wooden hand-held models. The beans are fed through a little door in the top of the box, and the ground coffee falls into a little drawer at the bottom. They are adjustable for any except the finest grind. Most look like Van Eyk-period Dutch, but are manufactured everywhere from Japan to Hoboken. Last time I checked, these wooden box-type grinders ranged in price from as little as $10 to as much as $50. The problems the box grinder offers are several: You can't get a grind fine enough for many coffee brewers, the grinding plates are small and inefficient, the handle is too short for good leverage, and worst of all, the grinder tends to slide around on the table. Nothing is so unnerving as a skittish grinder when you want a cup of coffee.

mounted hand grinders

Hand grinders which mount on the table or wall solve most of the problems posed by hand-held box grinders. They're much easier to use, adjust to finer grinds, and are much sturdier. I've already delivered my encomium to the Quaker City "OB" grain mill. The Spong hand mill is almost as large, sturdy, and efficient as the Quaker City mill, and a lot less in the way, since it can be screwed to the wall, and has a built-in receptacle to receive the ground coffee. Zassenhaus, a German firm, manufactures a lovely wall mill (around $60) with a pretty ceramic reservoir for the coffee beans. Unfortunately, it has some of the drawbacks of the hand-held mills: small grinding plates and a short handle with bad leverage.

electric burr grinders

On to the twentieth century. One type of electric grinder simply powers the same old burr or steel plates with electricity. The big grinders you see in grocery and coffee stores work on this principle. The household models have a receptacle for the coffee beans on top and one for the ground coffee at the bottom. You push a button and the coffee gets ground up in

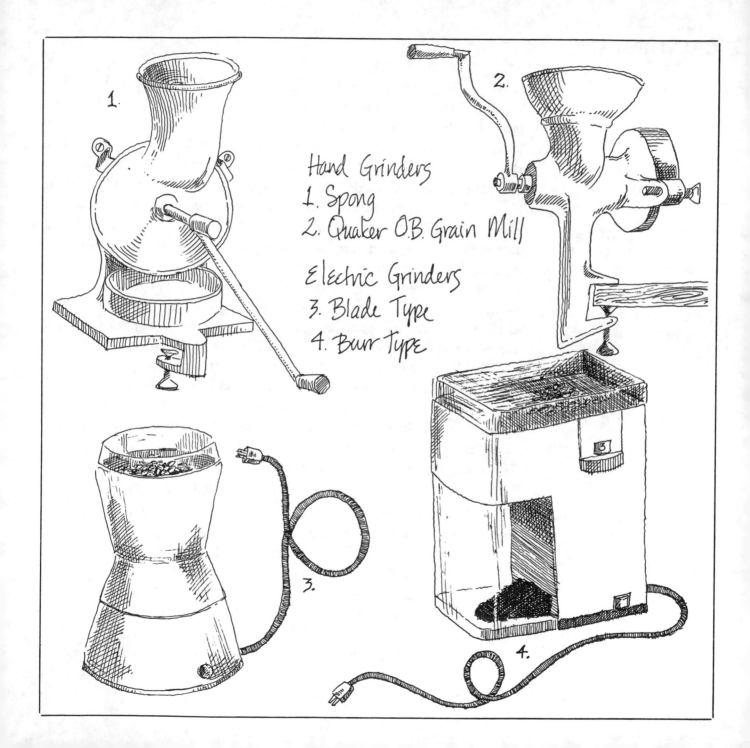

Hand Grinders
1. Spong
2. Quaker O.B. Grain Mill

Electric Grinders
3. Blade Type
4. Burr Type

between. These are good mills for genuinely lazy households and excellent for small firms who want to smarten up their coffee breaks with freshly ground coffee. One clear advantage to some of them is their relative cleanliness: Almost every other mill will spew at least a little ground coffee around the kitchen; these mills are fairly successful at keeping it to themselves.

The Braun "Aromatic" ($55) and the Krups "Grindmaster" ($55) are the best of the electric burr grinders I've tried, and either would be a good choice for lazy perfectionists for whom the OB Grain Grinder is too athletic. Both grind cool and will produce a fine and relatively uniform grind. Both have an automatic timing device. The Braun is easier to take apart and clean, and the beans feed more smoothly than in the Krups, which needs a little shake occasionally to keep them moving into the works. The advantages of the Krups are its clean good looks, a bracket for mounting on the wall, and a very clean delivery of ground coffee into the receptacle.

Other electric burr grinders: The Hobart KitchenAid ($65) is big, sturdy, and easy to service, but does not grind fine and has to be turned upside down to get at the grind adjustment. The receptacle that receives the coffee is open, allowing coffee chaff to escape the kitchen. The Salton mill ($40) grinds finer than the Hobart, but not as fine as the Braun or Krups. The measuring device on the Salton is a nuisance.

blade grinders

The third and last development in coffee grinding could only take place in an electrified society. Two steel blades whirr at extremely high speed at the bottom of a cup-like receptacle and literally knock the coffee beans to pieces. With the burr method the fineness of the grind is controlled by the distance between the plates, whereas with the blade method fineness is controlled by the length of time you let the blades whang away at your coffee. This makes the whole process a little hit and miss, unless you're so systematic you start timing yourself.

The disadvantages to the blade grinder? First, like the mortar and pestle, it doesn't make a uniform grind. Some of your coffee will be reduced to a caked-up powder around the edge of the grinder, and some will still be in relatively substantial chunks near the shaft of the blade. I don't think this matters all that much, however, unless you're into Turkish- or Middle Eastern-style coffee, in which case you should simply buy the Quaker City "OB" mill and forget all the other possibilities. Another drawback is the difficulty the blade grinder presents in getting the coffee out from under the little blades and into your brewer. You face the same problem when you clean your grinder.

The blade grinder's advantages are more succinctly stated: It is cheap, quick, and it doesn't take up much space in the kitchen. The numerous blade grinders on the market all appear to work equally well, differing only in speed and capacity. The new Braun ($28), manufactured in Spain, has a large capacity but seems to grind slowly; the new EVA ($28) has a smaller capacity but works faster; some specialty buyers recommend the Krups ($26) or Salton ($25).

cautions

You should be careful not to run your blade grinder continuously for more than a few seconds, since it will begin badly heating the ground coffee. If you make a fine grind, grind in spurts of about five seconds each. It also helps to gently bounce the bottom of the grinder on the counter between spurts to tumble the partly ground coffee back down around the blades.

HOW FINE?

In general, grind your coffee as fine as you can without clogging the holes or turning your coffee to mud. The finer the grind the more contact there will be between coffee and hot water, and the faster and more thoroughly the essential oils will be released, without further releasing harsher, less soluble chemicals.

On the other hand, you don't want a powder, because by completely pulverizing coffee you again destroy the essential oil; the heat and friction of the grinding process literally vaporizes it. Nor, of course, do you want to clog the holes in your coffee maker or filter or fill your cup with sediment.

Some brewing methods have special requirements. Both Middle Eastern coffee and espresso are special cases, as are open-pot and Melior or plunger-pot coffee. For details, see chapters 6 and 7.

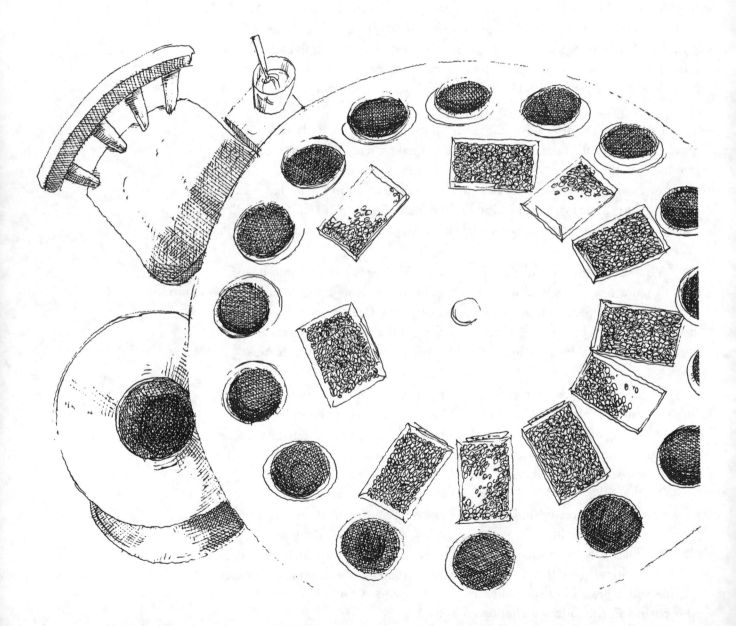

6 BREWING IT
Choosing a method and
a machine; brewing it right

NO MATTER what they're called, all ways of brewing coffee are basically the same: You soak the ground coffee in the water until the water tastes good and then you drink it. Nobody to my knowledge has figured out a different way to make coffee. And the only equipment you really need to make great coffee is an open pot, a flame, and possibly a strainer.

It's a tribute to human imagination and lust for perfection, however, that the simple act of combining hot water and ground coffee has produced so many ingenious variations, and occupied so many brilliant people for uncounted hours through the past three centuries. Thousands of coffee makers have been patented in the United States and Europe, but of this multitude only a handful have had any lasting effect or embodied any genuine innovation. The few bright ideas to achieve greatness can be divided according to three variables: how hot one makes the water; how one gets the water to the coffee; and how one separates the spent grounds from the brewed coffee.

three variables

Until the 18th century coffee was almost always boiled. Anyone who has read this far knows boiling damages coffee flavor because it vaporizes much of the coffee essence, while continuing to extract other bitter-tasting

BREWING IT

chemicals. The French began steeping, as opposed to boiling, their coffee in the early years of the 18th century, but this innovation did not penetrate the mainstream of coffee-drinking consciousness until the 19th century, and had to wait until the 20th to triumph. Today, all American and European methods favor hot (around 200°), as opposed to boiling, water.

water temperature

But if boiling water has been universally nixed, cold water has not. You can steep coffee in cold water and get substantially the same results as with hot water; the only difference is the process takes longer (several hours longer), and makes an extremely mild brew. Since reheating destroys flavor in coffee, cold-water coffee is made concentrated, and mixed with hot water like instant.

getting the water to the coffee

The second variable—how you get the water to your coffee—is a question of convenience. If you're in no hurry and want to hang around the kitchen, you might just as well heat the water in a pot and pour it over the coffee yourself. But if you want to get dressed, make love, or pet the cat while the coffee's brewing, then you might want a way to deliver the hot water to the coffee automatically. Furthermore, coffee making requires consistent and precise timing, a virtue difficult to maintain in our distracted age. The advantage to machines is their single-mindedness; they make coffee the same way every time, even if the phone rings.

The earliest effort at automation was the pumping percolator, originated in 1827 in France, the cradle of coffee-brewing invention. The French subsequently ignored it, but the United States, the cradle of convenience, adopted it enthusiastically. The pumping percolator uses the bubble power of boiling water to force little spurts of hot water up a tube and over the top of the coffee. The hot water, having seeped back through the coffee, returns to the reservoir to mix with the slowly bubbling water at the bottom of the pot. The process continues until the coffee is brewed.

Around 1840, the vacuum principle in coffee brewing was simultaneously discovered by several tinkerers, including a Scots naval engineer, Robert Napier. Napier's original looks more like a steam engine than a coffee maker, but as it has evolved today, the vacuum pot consists of two glass globes which fit tightly together, one above the other, with a cloth filter between. The ground coffee is placed in the upper globe, and water brought to boil in the lower. The two globes are fitted together and the heat lowered. Pressure developed by expanding water vapor in the lower globe forces the water into the upper, where it mixes with the ground coffee. After an interval of one to three minutes, the pot is removed from the heat and the light vacuum formed in the lower globe pulls the brewed coffee back down through the filter.

Finally, the 20th century has brought us both the automatic electric percolator, beloved of wedding guests, and the automatic filter-drip coffee maker, which holds the water in a reservoir above or next to the coffee, heats it, and measures it automatically over the ground coffee either by gravity or by the same bubble power that drives the percolator.

Now we reach the brewing operation which has stimulated coffee-pot tinkerers to their most extravagant efforts: the separation of brewed coffee from spent grounds. Again, original ideas are few, refinements endless. The Middle Easterner has the simplest solution: He simply lets most of the grounds settle to the bottom of the cup, and drinks the rest along with the brew. A very direct approach, like everything else about Middle Eastern coffee making. The original coffee drinkers, the Saudi Arabians, grind their beans more coarsely, and strain the coffee into the cup. This of course is a variation of the ubiquitous open-pot method, in which the consumer has the opportunity to invent his own methods for separating grounds from coffee.

separation of brew and grounds

The Arabian method was probably the earliest form of coffee brewing, the Middle Eastern or "Turkish" style having been developed later in Egypt. A third development took place in Vienna in 1684, after the lifting of the siege of Vienna, when Franz Georg Kolshitsky opened Central Europe's first cafe with coffee left behind by the routed Turks. Kolshitsky first tried to serve his booty Turkish style, but the Viennese wouldn't go for it. They called it "stewed soot," and continued to drink white wine and lager beer for breakfast. But when Kolshitsky started straining his coffee and serving it with milk and honey his success was assured; within a few years Vienna's great café tradition was well established. Strained or separated coffee has dominated European and American taste ever since.

An 18th-century Frenchman named De Belloy is credited with discovering the world's favorite method of separating coffee from grounds: the drip pot. Hot water is poured into an upper compartment with the coffee, and allowed to drip through a strainer or filter into a lower compartment, leaving the coffee grounds behind. An impressive variety of refinements has been developed since, including the Neapolitan flip pot, the cloth filter, and disposable paper filters.

One other method of separation deserves mention: After the coffee is steeped, a metal filter or strainer is forced *down through* the coffee like a plunger, squashing the coffee grounds to the bottom of the pot and leaving the clarified coffee above. There is no accepted generic name for this sort of brewer; we could call it a "plunger pot" which I like, or "Melior-type," after the French firm which popularized it.

GENERAL
CONSIDERATIONS
in buying a brewer

Your pot should ideally be made of glass or porcelain. Stainless steel will do. But if you have a choice in the matter, avoid aluminum. Food cooked in aluminum absorbs minute traces of the metal; coffee held for long in aluminum will develop a metallic flatness. When one adds to the danger to flavor the tendency of aluminum to pit and corrode, I think there is ample reason to avoid the metal in your coffee maker. Tin plate may also faintly taint coffee.

Your pot should be easy to clean. Coffee is oily, and allowed to accumulate this oil will eventually contribute a stale taste to fresh coffee. Stubborn brown stains in the corners can be soaked out with a strong solution of baking soda or one of the commercial urn cleaners on the market. Glass and porcelain are easiest to clean; aluminum and tin-coated metal the hardest. It is wise to avoid pots with seams or cracks, especially in the part which comes in direct contact with the brewed coffee. You might also check to make sure you can take the whole thing apart easily for an occasional thorough cleaning. In areas with alkaline, or hard water, a lime deposit will build up even in the parts of your maker which are untouched by coffee. The universal remedy is a strong solution of vinegar. Run it through the works of your brewer, and rinse thoroughly.

And now for the inevitable list of brewing rules and precepts. No matter whose invention you use to brew your coffee, I urge you to:

BREWING
SUGGESTIONS

- Use fresh coffee. Grind it as close to the moment you brew it as possible.
- Grind it as fine as you can make it without losing any through the holes in your coffee maker's filter, but never to an absolute powder. Melior and open-pot brewing require a less fine grind.
- Use plenty of coffee: at least two level tablespoons or one standard "coffee measure" per five- to six-ounce cup. You may want to use more, but I strongly suggest you never use less. Most mugs hold closer to eight ounces than six, so if you measure by the mug use two and a half to three level tablespoons for every mug of water. Coffee brewed strongly tastes better, and you can enjoy the distinction in your favorite coffee more clearly. If you brew with hard water or if you drink your coffee with milk, you should be especially careful to brew strong. If you feel that you're sensitive to caffeine, cut your coffee with caffeine-free beans (Chapter 9).
- Keep your coffee maker clean, and rinse it with hot water before you brew.
- Use fresh water, as free of impurities and alkalines as possible.
- Use hot water, as opposed to boiling or lukewarm water (Middle Eastern and cold-water coffee are exceptions). The Coffee Brewing

BREWING IT

Institute claims 200° is ideal. A rule of thumb: Bring the water to a boil and wait two minutes before pouring over the coffee.

• In filter and drip systems avoid brewing less than your brewer's full capacity: If the pot is made to brew six cups, your coffee will taste better if you brew the full six.

• Some don'ts: Don't boil coffee; it cooks off all the delicate flavoring essence, and leaves the bitter chemicals. Don't perk or reheat coffee; it has the same effect as boiling, only less so. Don't hold coffee for very long on the heat; same story. Don't mix old coffee with new; like using rotten wood to prop up a new building.

water quality Ninety-nine percent of a cup of coffee is water, and if you use bad, really bad, water, you might just as well throw away this book and buy a bottle of instant. The simple rule of thumb is this: If the water isn't pleasant to drink, don't make coffee with it. Use bottled or purified water. "Hard," or alkaline water will not directly harm flavor and aroma, but will mute some of the natural acids in coffee, and produce a blander cup without acidy snap. Water which has been treated with softeners makes even worse coffee, however, so if you do live in a hard water area you might either compensate by buying more acidy coffees (African, Arabian, and the best Indonesian and Central American growths), or again, brew with bottled water.

METHODS AND POTS

OPEN POT

The simplest brewing method, and as good as any. You steep the ground coffee in a pot of hot water, strain or otherwise separate the grounds from the brewed coffee, and serve. Open-pot coffee is a favorite of kinky individualists, hermits, hoboes, writers, artists, and other perennially light travelers. I have a sculptor friend who insists on making his in a pot improvised from a coffee can and a coat hanger. For such non-conformists, the real challenge is separating the grounds from the coffee without stooping to the aid of decadent bourgeois inventions like strainers.

Bring the cold water to a boil and let it cool for a minute or so. Toss in

Individual Cup
Drip

Automatic
filter Drip

Plunger-Pot

the coffee. Use a moderately fine grind, about what the stores call "drip." Stir gently to break up the lumps and let the mixture steep, covered, for two to four minutes. If you are willing to compromise, obtain a very fine mesh strainer; the best is made of nylon cloth. Strain the coffee and serve. If you consider yourself too authentic for a strainer, pour a couple of spoons of cold water over the surface of the coffee to sink whatever grounds have not already settled; in theory at least the cold water, which is heavier than the hot, will carry these stubbornly buoyant pieces with it to the bottom. If you wish to further clarify your coffee, put the shell of one egg into the pot with the coffee. The shell absorbs some of the sediment which clouds the brew.

For the lazy or less resourceful, I recommend a little nylon bag ($3 to $4) that sits inside the traditional straight-sided coffee pot, supported on the outside by a plastic ring. You put the ground coffee in the nylon bag and pour hot water over it. In two to four minutes you simply lift the bag and grounds out of the brew.

PLUNGER

This is essentially open-pot coffee with a sexy method for separating the grounds from the brew. The pot is a narrow glass cylinder. A fine-meshed screen plunger fits tightly inside the cylinder; you put a fine-ground coffee in the cylinder, pour boiling water over it, and insert the plunger in the top of the cylinder without pushing it down. After about four minutes the coffee will be thoroughly steeped and you push the plunger down through the coffee, clarifying it and forcing the grounds to the bottom of the pot. You serve the coffee directly from the cylinder. Be certain not to use too fine a grind unless you have an athlete or a weight-lifter at the table; the plunger will become almost impossible to push down through the coffee.

French Melior

The cheapest plunger-style coffee brewer is the difficult-to-find Booton-ware "Insta-Brewer," a six-cup model that retails for around $20. It's neither as sturdy nor as classy as the French Melior metal and glass models, but the price is right, and I wouldn't call it ugly. The French Melior makers put out a deco-looking plastic-frame six-cup model for about $33, a very dignified (and expensive) traditional-look model in flameproof glass with a rhodium-plate frame for $56 (three-cup) to $74 (12-cup), and for the truly extravagant, a model nearly entirely sheathed in rhodium plate (it looks like an accessory from a Rolls Royce and is in the Design Collection of the Museum of Modern Art) at well over $100.

Both open-pot and plunger-style coffee tend to be rich in sediment, oils, and minute globs of gelatinous stuff which neither settle nor dissolve, which chemists call colloids. Coffee made by the filter method has far less of this stuff; filter coffee brewed by the cold-water method has least of all. Some people prefer their coffee as clear and free from such minute muck as possible; such purists should choose a filter brewer. But for those of us who like the heavier body and richer, more idiosyncratic flavor of coffee *with* the muck, open pot or plunger-style brewing is a good choice.

The question of muck aside, advantages of the plunger pot are its value as a conversation piece, its portability (you can brew coffee at the table rather than messing around with filters and such in the kitchen), and the relative speed of the operation, which means hotter coffee than you get with the drip or filter method. It is, however, a bit harder to clean than most drip or filter pots.

DRIP

The drip pot was invented by a Frenchman around 1800 and popularized by Count Rumford, an eccentric American who became a Count of the Holy Roman Empire, married two rich widows, the second one French, and spent much of his leisure time making enemies and coffee. The drip maker typically consists of two compartments, an upper and lower, divided by a metal or ceramic "filter," or strainer. The ground coffee is placed in the upper compartment and hot water poured over it. The brewed coffee trickles through the strainer into the lower compartment.

A very attractive porcelain drip pot, with an elegant, traditionally French silhouette, can be bought at specialty stores for anywhere from $30 to $50. The French also make individual one-cup drip coffee makers which

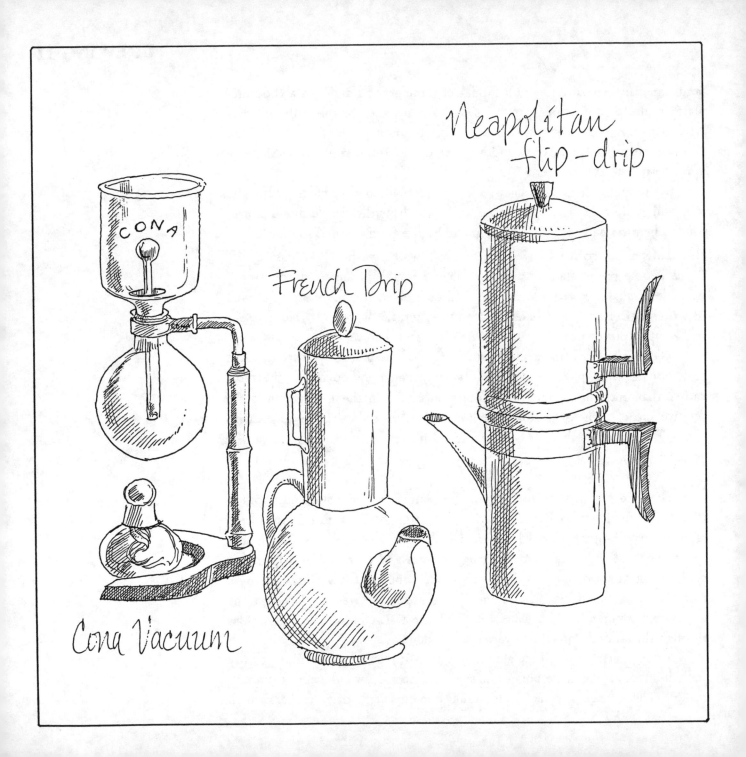

Neapolitan flip-drip

French Drip

CONA

Cona Vacuum

fit over the cup. You fill the top with hot water and the coffee drips directly into the cup.

A popular variation of the drip pot was invented in 1819 by Marize, a French tinsmith. This is the reversible, double, or flip-drip pot, which has since been adopted by the Italians as the "Neapolitan" pot. Rather than being laid loosely on top of the strainer, as in the regular drip pot, the ground coffee is secured in a two-sided strainer at the waist of the pot. The water is heated in one side of the pot, then the whole thing is flipped over, and the hot water drips through the coffee into the other, empty side. There are several versions of the Neapolitan machinetta, or flip-drip pot, available. An aluminum version is the cheapest—around $8 for the smallest, up to $10 for the largest. Since aluminum is not a desirable material for coffee brewers, I recommend instead one of the several attractive copper versions at around $30, or a modern-look stainless, also at $30.

Neapolitan flip-drip

Use as fine a grind of coffee as possible in your drip brewer. If the holes clog or you find appreciable sediment in your cup, try a slightly coarser grind. Handle the water as you would with any other brewing system: Bring it to boiling, let it sit for one to two minutes, then pour it *slowly* over the coffee, making sure you have saturated all the grounds. Cover to preserve heat. Mix the coffee lightly after it has brewed, since the first coffee to drip through is stronger and heavier than the last. Both drip and filter coffees often cool excessively during the brewing process; it helps to preheat the bottom half of the pot with hot tap water before brewing. If that isn't enough, buy a heat-reducing pad and keep your pot on the stove while you're brewing. If you're troubled by sediment, disposable cloth filters are available to fit most drip brewers.

saturate
all the grounds

One of the best things about drip coffee making are the one-cup models that fit directly over the cup and allow you to make a single cup of delicious, fresh-brewed coffee in about the same amount of time it would take to make yourself a cup of flat, odorless instant. The one-cup Rittergold, with gold-plated mesh filter, goes for about $8; a one-cup drip maker in aluminum can be bought for as little as $2; ceramic styles sell for around $6.

PERCOLATOR

Until recently, the pop of a pumping percolator at work producing coffee ranked along with the acceleration of a well-tuned car as one of North America's best-loved sounds. However, the pumping percolator is probably the one brewing device you will *not* find in your neighborhood specialty store. However reassuring the sensuous gurgle of a percolator is psychologically, chemically it means only one thing: You're boiling your coffee, and prematurely vaporizing the delicate flavoring oils. Every pop of the percolator means another bubble of aroma and flavor is bursting at the top of the pot, bestowing its gift on your kitchen rather than on your palate.

Opinions differ as to the extent of the damage the percolator inflicts on coffee flavor. *Consumer Reports* magazine (September 1974) served coded cups of drip and percolator coffee both to "experts" and to its staff. The experts unanimously and consistently preferred the drip coffee to the perked coffee, but the staff's reaction was mixed. I find I can invariably pick out perked coffee in a similar test by the slightness of its aroma and a flat, slightly bitter edge to the flavor.

If you must have a pumping percolator, a good electric is probably the best choice, since the heat is automatically controlled to produce a perk rather than a boil, and most electrics have a thermostat which should reduce the heat at the optimum moment to prevent overextraction.

VACUUM

Coffee made by the vacuum method does not differ markedly from coffee made with the filter cone, and since the manipulations involved are a bit more complex than those demanded by the filter method, the vacuum pot has lost considerable popularity since its heyday in the twenties and thirties. But for some the leisurely and alchemical shifting of liquids in the two glass globes has a continuing appeal, and the coffee produced should be as good as any.

Vacuum brewers are difficult to find in these hurried days. The one you will most likely run across in specialty stores is either the Cona Table Model ($70 to $80), a British product that looks like an elegant piece of laboratory equipment lifted from Captain Nemo's submarine, or the French Hellem ($90 to $120), a similarly romantic design with a lighter Gallic touch. Both brew coffee at the table by means of a spirit lamp, and after several minutes of exquisitely complex maneuvers will produce two or three cups of excellent coffee, brewed by impeccable filter principles. The water, by the way, should be preheated before being placed in the globe, since the spirit lamp, however picturesque, is excruciatingly slow in bringing cold water to brewing temperature.

Coffee-pot tinkerers started using cloth filters around 1800; disposable paper filters came later, and were never really popular until after World War II. The main objection to paper filters then and now: They must be continually replaced. The main objection to cloth filters: They get dirty and are difficult to clean. In our disposable age the paper filter has triumphed, but as thrifty times return, cloth, in the form of new synthetics, may yet make a comeback.

FILTER

Nearly all filter coffee makers work the same way. A paper filter is placed in a pastic, glass, or ceramic holder; fine-ground (a fine grit just short of powdery) coffee goes in the filter, and the filter container goes atop a flameproof glass or ceramic flask. From there you proceed as you do for drip coffee.

The advantages of filter brewing: It permits you to use a very fine grind of coffee and effect a quick and thorough extraction, and the paper filters make grounds easy to dispose of and your coffee maker easy to keep clean. Because of their simplicity and popularity, coffee cones are the cheapest coffee brewing devices on the market. Those who like a light-bodied clear coffee free of oils, colloids, and sediment will enjoy a good filter coffee; those who like a heavier, richer brew will prefer other methods.

advantages

The disadvantages: Paper filters slow the drip process to such a degree that the coffee may require warming before drinking. And, though your initial investment in the cone may be small, you'll be paying for filters for the rest of your coffee-drinking career. The first of these disadvantages can be gotten round: Lukewarm coffee can be avoided by keeping your pot over low heat buffered by a heat-reducing device or a hot water bath, or on an electric warmer. The expense of paper filters can be avoided by purchasing a reuseable cloth filter available in specialty stores for about $3, but I don't recommend these compromise filters; they take too much out of the coffee and are hard to keep clean. I might add that filter coffee tastes best when *more the* brewed in large quantities; the big restaurant urns that take a pound of *better* ground coffee at a time brew splendid coffee; an eight-cup filter brewer will make very good coffee; a one-cup filter cone tends to make a weak, mediocre cup no matter what you do. This phenomenon of diminishing return in proportion to diminishing filter brewer size is well known in the coffee trade; what causes it I'm not certain, but I suspect it has something to do with the relatively greater proportion of filter paper surface to ground coffee in the smaller brewers. The filter paper simply seems to dominate the coffee in a one-cup cone, filtering out too many of the flavorful oils along with the sediment.

A last point, which needs to be said carefully: If one runs hot water through most filter papers and tastes the hot water afterwards, the sensitive palate will detect a faint "papery" taste. Whatever produces this taste is without a doubt harmless to health, and could hardly harm the flavor of a robust cup of coffee. As a matter of fact, I can't imagine it adversely affecting the taste of even the most lackluster, insipid cup of coffee. But the taste is there, and if you're the kind of person who insists on feeling peas under mattresses, you may want to make the taste test described above and decide whether you care to switch to another brewing method.

There is an enormous array of filter brewers on the market. One has a choice of material (as always, glass and ceramic are the best) and of filter shape, which runs from the simple cone, to the Melitta-style pocket or wedge, to the flat-bottomed "basket" filter. Theoretically the basket filter provides the most even and most thorough extraction, since with both the cone and wedge only the coffee at the bottom of the filter comes into repeated contact with the brewing water.

In practice, however, there doesn't appear to be any difference among coffees made with the three styles of filter. Other factors, such as coffee quality, water quality, water temperature, and the care taken in pouring the water over the ground coffee, appear to be more important than filter shape.

Among brewers using the cone-shaped filters, the most famous is the Chemex, the original American filter brewer that was developed from, and still resembles, a well-made piece of laboratory equipment. Many will find its austere design (honored by the Museum of Modern Art) and authentic materials (glass and wood in the traditional models) attractive, but the single-piece hourglass shape makes cleaning difficult. The blown-glass models with wood handles range from $25 to $35; the molded glass models with plastic handles sell for about half that. Most of the Chemex accessories match the traditional brewer in elegance. My favorite is the copper water bath ($15) for keeping the coffee warm while brewing. The Rockline, another brewer using cone-shaped filters, is the cheapest filter set available. The two- to eight-cup plastic cone with 12 filters sells for around $2; the matching flameproof glass flask goes for around $5, and the filters for about $1.75 a hundred.

Chemex

The Melitta company, the originator of the wedge-shaped pocket filter, makes a set for almost every pocketbook; the top of their line is an all-porcelain set with a classic silhouette for $22 for the smallest to $53 for the largest. At the other end is a clear plastic cone and matching flameproof flask for $5 to $8. The compact, attractive Melitta electric warmer costs around $16. Melitta filters cost about $3.75 a hundred, which is 1½ cents more per filter than the cheapest competitors, the Rockline. The Hammarplast "Koffi" set ($27) is an assertively colorful thermos with a matching

Melitta

Melitta-style cone. And if you already have a serving thermos, Melitta makes a cone ($5) that will probably fit it.

Single-cup filter cones fit directly over your cup. Melitta makes a one-cup filter cone for about $2; others are a quarter or two less. As I mentioned earlier I find the filter paper overly dominates the coffee in these very small brewers, and I would suggest you make your single-cup brewer a drip model.

Careful brewing can make considerable difference in the quality of filter coffee. Bring cold water to just short of boiling and pour just a little over the grounds, making sure all the coffee gets wet. Pour the rest of the water through, and stir the coffee lightly after brewing. If you make a small quantity, less than four cups, you may want to use slightly more ground coffee to compensate for the flavor lost to the filter.

AUTOMATIC FILTER DRIP

The latest thing in the coffee world. In 1973, two hundred thousand automatic filter drip coffee makers were sold in the United States. In 1974, that figure rose to three million, and doubled to six million in 1975. Today, the automatic filter drip has virtually eliminated the electric percolator from the market in larger cities. Either America is in love with a new gimmick, or the American coffee drinker always did consider filter coffee better, but clung to the percolator because it saved time and steps.

The heart of the automatic filter drip system is the familiar filter, receptacle, and decanter. The machine simply heats water to the optimum heat for coffee brewing and automatically measures it into the filter. The coffee drips into the decanter, and an element under the decanter keeps the coffee hot once it is brewed. The consumer measures cold water into the top of the maker, measures coffee into the filter, presses a switch, and in from four to eight minutes has four to 12 cups of coffee.

Sounds terrific, doesn't it? Nevertheless, the latest systematic inquiry into the worth of the automatic filter drip machines, a *Consumer Reports* article (January 1980), rates coffee produced by only one of the 23 machines tested as totally satisfactory, and coffee from only four more as better than average. The other 18 machines made coffee rated either mediocre in body and flavor or outright defective: flat, weak, bitter or harsh. My own experience with these machines confirms the *CR* findings: Most make a weak, lackluster cup. For a variety of technical reasons they do not extract enough of the good stuff from the coffee.

Still, the best automatic filter brewers produce a coffee far superior in flavor to percolator coffee, and they produce it with precision and consistency. A conscientious shopper out to beat the odds and buy that best possible automatic filter brewer faces a considerable challenge, however. In addition to the slippery question of brew quality, there are a multitude of design variables to consider: Does the water reservoir have a dust cover? Is the filter receptacle easy to insert and remove? (Brewers in which the receptacle sits on top of the decanter are usually easier to use.) Is the decanter easy to clean? (Straight-sided decanters with large mouths are better than rounded ones with small mouths.) Does the brewer have an on-off switch or do you have to unplug it to turn it off? Can you interrupt the brewing process to pour a cup or two or do you have to wait until the last drop drips? How long does the brewing process take? Does the brewer give you the option of brewing without filters? (Some brewers have a built-in nylon mesh filter.) Is the receptacle that holds the filter and the coffee ample enough to sustain the bubbling up that occurs when you use a fresh coffee? Since no automatic filter brewer rates a positive answer to all these questions, the serious consumer has to set his priorities and shop accordingly.

a shopping challenge

Specific recommendations are difficult, not only because of the many design variables, but because manufacturers drop old models and add new ones almost yearly. Nevertheless here are some notes:

recommendations

Braun: The original Braun Aromaster KF20 (around $80) was consistently praised for coffee quality by retailers, and was the only automatic brewer *Consumer Reports* found to yield a totally satisfactory cup. The warming plate didn't keep the coffee hot enough for North American tastes, however, and whether for this reason or others the manufacturer has discon-

Braun

tinued it. At this writing it is available in only a few stores. Its replacement, the Braun KF35 ($80), is an almost totally new design, and though it seems to me to brew just as good a cup as the old model, it has not been on the market long enough for anyone to recommend it without reservation.

Krups

Krups: The compact, good-looking Krups 261A ($70) brewed a better than average cup for the *CR* tasters; most specialty shop buyers also like the Krups line, which boasts an impressive list of special features, including a device that allows you to interrupt brewing to pour, a classy digital timer on the TS8 ($150) that will wake you up with fresh coffee, and a model with a serving thermos in place of decanter ($80).

Proctor-Silex

Proctor-Silex A301N ($40): Brews better than average coffee according to *CR*.

Farberware

Farberware 265 ($40): Another inexpensive American-made brewer with a *CR* better-than-average rating; technically a clean and straightforward machine; visually a neo-colonial plastic blunder.

Norelco

Norelco: *CR* gave coffee brewed in the Norelco HB5140 ($40) its better than average rating. The American-made Norelco brewers are good-looking and relatively inexpensive. The HB5180 ($60) has a digital timer and costs approximately $90 less than its somewhat fancier Krups competitor. The HB5123 "Expresso" is a cute little brewer that makes one to four cups. The main complaint about Norelco brewers among coffee specialists is the size of the receptacle: It is too small in the larger (8- to 12-cup) models, making it impossible to use a fresh, fine-ground coffee (which bubbles up owning to freed gases) without causing flooding. Most also find the "Dial-A-Brew" strength-control feature annoying and pointless.

West Bend

West Bend: *CR* gave coffee from the West Bend QuikDrip a mediocre rating. Many specialty shop owners swear by it however; I find it makes as good a cup as any and better than most. The older "QuikDrip" model ($45) has an optional nylon filter and so can be used without paper; the newer "FlavoDrip" ($45) does not retain this useful feature. In appearance both models are overweight and frumpy.

Melitta: The Melitta automatic brewers, five models ranging from a ten-cup at $45 to a one-cup "Personal" brewer at $25, were not tested by *CR*, although their tasters gave a pour-over Melitta, used by way of comparison, a top rating. I find that the Melitta machines, an ordinary-looking lot, make a good cup, and specialty shop buyers seem satisfied. *Melitta*

Chemex: Not tested by *CR*. Good marks by specialty buyers. Cleanly designed both technically and aesthetically, though the combined brewer-decanter, as noted earlier, is difficult to clean. *Chemex*

Mr. Coffee: Poor rating for coffee quality from *CR*; all three models tested made coffee with a variety of defects. Some annoying design flaws as well. *Mr. Coffee*

Bunn: Bad marks from *CR* and even more design problems. *Bunn*

If I were to go out on a limb on all this, I would recommend that you pour the water over the coffee yourself and forget about these $40-and-up plastic robots. But if convenience counts for you, at least get a good automatic brewer with a big receptacle and grind your coffee as fine as possible within the manufacturer's suggested limits in order to obtain the maximum extraction possible.

The Toshiba "My Cafe" ($80) is in a category all its own. It is an anomaly in two respects. It does not take paper filters, making it an automatic drip rather than automatic filter drip, and, more spectacularly, it grinds *and* brews coffee *in the same receptacle.* You measure whole coffee beans into the brewing basket, lock on a cover, turn on the grinder control for 15 or 20 seconds, and a pair of blades knocks apart the coffee. You next switch to "brew," whereupon hot water bubbles over the ground coffee and drips through a stainless steel filter into the decanter. No messy transfer of ground coffee from grinder to brewer; it all happens in the same place. *Toshiba grinder-brewer*

The Toshiba is good-looking, compact, and for a small capacity brewer (four 5-ounce cups) makes decent to good coffee. At this writing it is brand new to both the Japanese and the North American markets. Perhaps by the time this edition is into its second printing the Toshiba "My Cafe" will be a household word, with the market inundated by imitations, and North Americans will have moved their coffee drinking habits still another notch up from the pumping percolator.

But I doubt it. The concept seems a bit fussy and complex, and since you can't watch the coffee as it's being ground, you have to time the procedure with a second hand, an awkward and haphazard approach at best. Such design flaws can be overcome, however, and given the American love of gadgets this one conceivably could follow Cuisinart, Mr. Coffee, and toaster ovens into our hearts and kitchens.

CONCENTRATE
METHODS

In Latin America as well as in many other parts of the world, a very strong concentrated coffee is brewed, stored, and added in small amounts to hot water or milk to make a sort of pre-industrial instant. It is possible to obtain a strong concentrate with almost any brewing method, although only one, the cold-water method, has obtained much popularity in the United

hot water

States. To make a hot-water concentrate, use eight cups of water to a pound of finely ground coffee and brew in your customary fashion. If your coffee maker won't handle a pound at a time, halve the recipe or brew twice. Store the resulting concentrate in a stoppered bottle in the refrigerator, and in a preheated cup, add about one ounce to every five ounces of hot water. A shot glass holds an ounce, and makes a convenient measure.

cold water

The "cold-water" concentrate method has been adopted by two manufacturers, Filtron and Toddy. Both make an excellent cold-water brewer for around $18. Filtron also makes a Deluxe model for about $32, which appears to be little more than an older, more expensive version of their Filtron Jr. All three work substantially the same way: You steep a pound of regular grind coffee in eight cups of cold water for anywhere from 10 to 20 hours, filter the resulting concentrate into a separate container, store it in the refrigerator, and add it, an ounce to a cup, to hot water.

The result is a very mild, delicate brew, with little acidity (of either good or bad variety), light body, a natural sweetness, and an evanescent, muted flavor. Someone who takes his coffee weak and black, and likes a delicate flavor free of acid highlights and the rest of the idiosyncracies of coffee flavor, may well like the cold-water method. Those who for medical reasons require a milder brew also might find it suitable. And it is, like the hot concentrate, convenient.

But anyone who likes strong coffee, distinctive coffee, or coffee with milk would be better off doing it another way. Another problem: If you combine an ounce or more of refrigerated concentrate with five ounces of hot water, you end with a mixture a little less than scalding hot; add milk and your coffee is virtually lukewarm.

Some people like to use cold-water concentrate in cooking, but I prefer a hot-water concentrate because the coffee flavor is stronger and more distinctive; cold-water concentrate makes everything taste like store-bought coffee ice cream. The same can be said for using cold-water concentrate in cold coffee drinks; one needs a concentrate for cold drinks to compensate for ice dilution, but some (like me) prefer the more distinctive punch of hot-brewed concentrate.

You don't have to buy a cold-water brewer to enjoy cold-water coffee, although the store-bought brewers are much more convenient than any expedient. To improvise you need a glass bowl, a large coffee cone and filter, and a bottle with an airtight closure (snap-on plastic won't do) in which to refrigerate the finished concentrate. Take a pound of your favorite coffee, regular grind. You can use any coffee, any roast. Chuck it in the bowl, and add eight cups of cold water. Poke the floating coffee down into the water so all the grounds are wet; then let the bowl stand in a cool, dark corner for anywhere from 10 to 20 hours, depending on how strong you want your concentrate. When the brewing period is over, use your cone to filter the concentrate into the second, airtight container, and store in the refrigerator For hot coffee, use one to two ounces per cup.

improvising a brewer

Any concentrate will keep its flavor for months if the bottle is tightly capped, but your best bet is to make only as much as you will drink in a

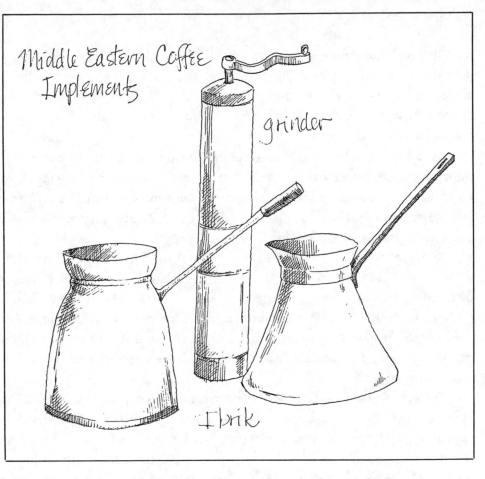

Middle Eastern Coffee Implements

grinder

Ibrik

week or two. The cold water Toddy people say you can freeze the concentrate, but I've found it loses some much-needed flavor, and I suggest you simply halve the recipe if you can't drink a pound's worth in two weeks.

MIDDLE EASTERN
Turkish, Greek

Middle Eastern coffee is most often called "Turkish" coffee in this country, but this is a misnomer. For one thing, it is drunk all over the Middle East, not only in Turkey, and if a patriotic Greek or Armenian serves it to you, you had better *not* call it Turkish coffee. Secondly, according to all accounts the method was invented in Cairo and later spread from there to Turkey and Istanbul. Middle Eastern coffee is unique, first, because some of the coffee grounds are deliberately drunk along with the coffee, and second, because the coffee is usually brewed *with* sugar, rather than sweetened after brewing. Tiny grains of coffee float suspended in the sweetened liquid, imparting a heavy, almost syrupy weight to the cup.

It's possible to make good, flavorful Middle Eastern-style coffee in any old pot; the investment you make in brewing equipment is more important to ritual and esthetics than flavor. But, as I find myself pointing out so often, ritual seems to be as important as flavor in the life of coffee. So if you want to be authentic you'll need one of those small, conical pots (it looks a little like an inverted megaphone) called an *ibrik* (Turkish) or *briki* (Greek). *ibrik* The best and most authentic are made of copper or brass and tinned inside, and cost anywhere from $10 to $20. You should also have demitasse cups and saucers; the standard restaurant variety of brown or plain white porcelain is fine, and can be bought at any large restaurant-supply store.

The most important piece of functional equipment in making Middle Eastern-style coffee is the grinder. Since you drink the grounds, and you *grinder* don't want to be picking grains of coffee from between your teeth, you need a very fine, uniform grind, a dusty powder in fact. Only the best home mills will produce such a grind. The Quaker City OB grain mill works very, very well. A Middle Eastern-style grinder (the kind that looks like a tall pepper mill) works well but rather slowly. Some burr-type electric mills (the Braun, for example) produce a good Middle Eastern grind coffee, but "cook" the coffee with friction.

Of course there are pre-ground Middle Eastern coffees available, both in cans and pre-wrapped at your specialty coffee store. Few specialty stores can grind true Middle Eastern coffee for you fresh, by the way; their grinders do not as a rule adjust that fine. They have it pre-ground, which puts it about in the same class as canned coffees.

The roast you choose is a matter of taste, as is the provenance of the coffee. Most "Turkish" or Middle Eastern-style coffee sold in the States is a fairly dark roast, the sort most stores sell as Italian. A blend of a winey coffee like Kenya or Mocha, some Sumatran, and a good dark French roast makes an excellent Middle Eastern coffee.

kaimaki

Authentic Middle Eastern coffee should have a thin head of brown foam completely covering the surface of the coffee. In Greece, this is called the *kaimaki,* and to serve coffee without it is an insult to the guest and a disgrace to the host. A Greek friend of mine tells about her mother secretly struggling in their kitchen to produce a good head of *kaimaki,* while the rest of the family nervously diverted the guests with small talk in the parlor. In America, the *kaimaki* is usually dispensed with, for the simple reason that it's very difficult to produce. Your Middle Eastern coffee should taste good the first time you make it, and the foam can wait until you're an expert.

sweetening

Never plan to fill the *ibrik* to more than one-half its capacity. You need the other half to accommodate the foam which will boil up from the coffee. Start by measuring two level-to-rounded teaspoons of freshly ground, powdered coffee per demitasse into the *ibrik.* Add about one level teaspoon of sugar for every teaspoon of coffee. This makes a coffee a Greek would call "sweet"; add one and a half teaspoons of sugar per teaspoon of coffee and you get "heavy sweet"; a half teaspoon is "light sweet"; add no sugar and you're serving your coffee plain, or *sketo.*

brewing

Now measure the water into the *ibrik.* Stir to dissolve the sugar, then turn on the heat, medium to high. After a while the coffee will begin to gently boil. Let it, but watch it closely. Eventually the foam, which should have a darkish crust on top, will begin to climb the narrowing part of the *ibrik.* When it fills the flare at the top of the pot and is at the point of boiling over, turn off the flame. Immediately, and gently, so as not to settle the foam, pour into the cups. Fill each cup halfway first, then return to add some foam to each. Again, even though you may fail with the foam, the coffee will always be delicious.

Middle Easterners like to add all sorts of spices to their coffee. The preferred spice, however, and the one I suggest you try, is cardamom. Grind the cardamom seeds as finely as you grind the coffee, and put them in with the coffee and sugar right at the beginning. There are usually three seeds in a cardamom pod; start by adding the equivalent of *one seed* (not pod) per demitasse of water, or a "pinch" if the cardamom is pre-ground.

One can hardly call making instant coffee brewing, and I don't have a chapter on mixing and stirring, so I'll have to put my discussion of instant coffees here, as a sort of exemplary afterthought.

INSTANT COFFEE
a word (no more)

I don't wish to insinuate that instant coffee producers are terrible men in tall hats and vests who sneak around in their limousines ripping off the public's birthright—a rich, fragrant cup of real coffee. Instant coffee technologists seem quite passionately involved in their quest for a better instant coffee. And at first glance (not taste) instant coffee does seem to offer many advantages: It stays fresh longer; you can't mess it up as badly as you can regular coffee; it's fast, easy, and clean; it can be mixed by the cup to individual taste; it contains somewhat less caffeine than regularly brewed coffee; and because the instant process neutralizes strong or unusual flavors, the manufacturer can get away with cheaper beans and pass his savings on to the consumer. Without a doubt some instant coffee is the least expensive caffeine high around; it's the coffeeholic's answer to cheap port.

Yet few of these well-publicized advantages prove out. Instant does stay fresher, but grinding your own makes an even fresher cup. Instant is cleaner, but so are TV dinners. And true, it's hard to blow a cup of instant, but if you've read this far you're all experts anyhow. And if it's only speed you're looking for, cold-water concentrate or the one-cup drip I described earlier will give you much better coffee, and just as fast. So for people with ordinary intelligence who have a tongue and a nose, I can't see any reasons except *possibly* cleanliness and a slight edge in price to recommend instant.

dubious advantages

And you don't need it on backpacking or canoeing trips either—open-pot coffee works fine in the wilds and adds no more weight than instant. At five in the morning after brushing the earwigs out of your sleeping bag and

BREWING IT

cleaning up the mess the raccoons made, you *need* a real cup of coffee. About the only advantage to instant is it doesn't attract bears.

Finally, for those who like unusual coffees, dark-roast coffees, in fact, anyone who wants anything except the standard American cup, instant coffee offers *no* viable alternatives. As I pointed out earlier, the "exotic" *insipid fabrications* instant coffee mixes currently in the supermarkets are insipid fabrications; by comparison freeze-dried Colombian is a superior beverage. If you crave variety, you must go back to basics.

Once we dismiss the advantages of instant, the advantages of brewed-from-scratch stand out in aromatic taste-tingling relief. Why does instant often taste more like liquid taffy than coffee? The key again is the extremely volatile coffee essence, which provides all the aroma of fresh coffee and most of the flavor. Remember that this oil is developed by roasting, and remains sealed up in little packets in the bean until liberated by grinding and brewing. Once the coffee essence hits the water, it doesn't last long, which is the reason coffee that sits for a while tastes so flat.

Now instant coffee is brewed pretty much the way a gourmet would do it at home: The beans are roasted, immediately ground, and brewed in gigantic percolators, filter urns really. But, when that fresh, hot stuff is dehydrated, what happens? Remember, "dehydrate" means take the water out, and with the water goes—yes, the coffee essence, the minute little droplets of flavor and odor that mean the difference between flavorless, bitter brown water and coffee.

But here technology comes clanking over the hill to save the day. If you *putting the flavor back* lose the flavor somewhere along the line, well then we better *put it back in again.* Coffee technologists have long known that a lot of the essential oil literally goes up in smoke out the chimneys of their roasters. So—you guessed it. The instant coffee people condense some of the essential oil lost in roasting, and *put it back in the coffee* just before it's packed. Clever? Also tricky. So much so that even according to industry admissions, the sharp

116

corners of coffee flavor are neutralized—in other words, the instant process makes bad coffee beans taste better, and *good* coffee beans taste bad.

So far I've stuck to concretes like efficiency and price, and fairly clear subjectives, like flavor and aroma. But I feel obligated to add that the ritual of making a true cup of coffee the right way every morning is good for the soul. It cuts down on mindless coffeeholism, and helps to steady the heart for the more complex activities to come. It gets you started with a confident sense that you can at least make a cup of coffee right, and it's always best to start out winning.

"Which brewing method is best?" is a naive question. "Which brewing method is best for me?" is a question to which one can at least approximate an answer. Take just two variables, body and convenience. Coffee made by the Middle Eastern method is heaviest in body, espresso next heaviest, and cold-water coffee lightest in body, with plain filter coffee a close second. Between are ranged the coffees produced by all the other methods: open pot, plunger pot, drip, and so on. Who is to say which is "best"?

WHICH IS BEST?

Even the question of convenience is relative. The cold-water method is clearly most convenient, automatic filter drip close, and Middle Eastern and open pot a remote last. Still, no one can tell my sculptor friend that making coffee without a strainer in a coffee can is bad because it is clumsy and inconvenient; he appreciates the inconvenience; it adds to his satisfaction and takes his mind off the anxieties of his work. One of the principal reasons for drinking coffee in the first place is the esthetic satisfaction of ritual. You ought to not only love the coffee your pot makes, but the pot itself, and all the little things you do with it.

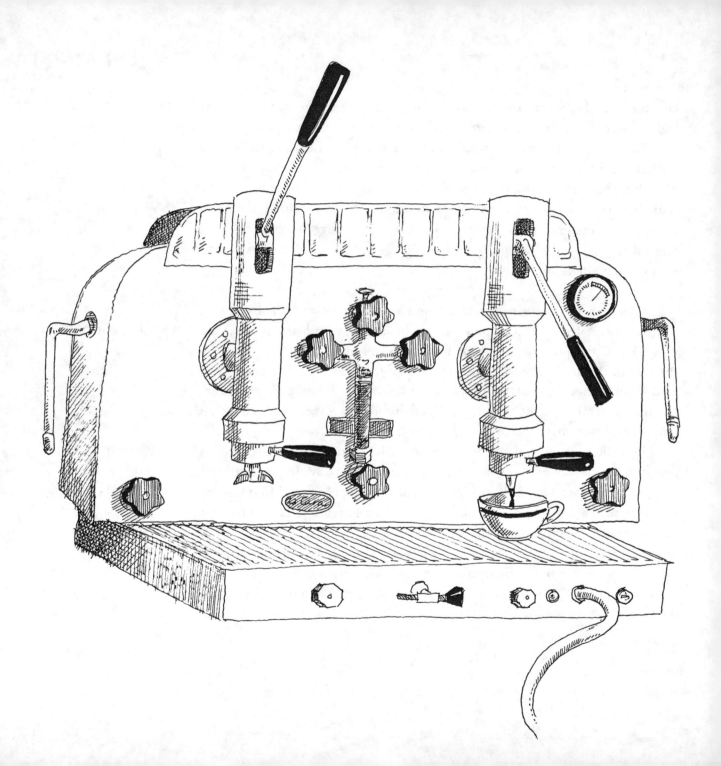

7 ESPRESSO
What it is and how to brew it

ESPRESSO IS several things all at once. It is a unique method of coffee brewing in which hot water is forced under pressure through tightly packed coffee, a cup at a time. It is a roast of coffee, darker brown than the normal American roast, but not quite black. In a larger sense, it is an entire approach to coffee cuisine, involving not only roast and brewing method, but grind and grinder, a technique of heating milk, and a traditional menu of drinks. And in the largest sense of all, it is an atmosphere or mystique: The espresso brewing machine is the spiritual heart and esthetic centerpiece of the European-style café.

an atmosphere or mystique

The espresso system was developed in and for cafés; despite advances in inexpensive home espresso systems one still can not duplicate the finest café espresso or cappuccino in one's kitchen or dining room. You can come close, however, and I discuss the strategy of the attempt in later pages. For now, I want to address myself to the big, shiny café machines.

Fundamentally they make coffee like any other brewer: by steeping ground coffee in hot water. The difference is the *pressure* applied to the hot water. In normal brewing processes the water seeps by gravity down through

ESPRESSO

ground coffee loosely laid over a filter; in the espresso process the water is *forced under pressure* through very finely ground coffee packed tightly over the filter.

advantages of
the espresso system

A fast, yet thorough brewing makes the best coffee. If hot water and ground coffee stay in contact too long, the more unpleasant chemicals in the coffee will be extracted, and the pleasant aroma and flavor will evaporate. Hence the superiority of the espresso system: The pressurized water makes almost instant contact with every grain of ground coffee, and just as instantly begins dribbling out into the cup. Another advantage to the café espresso system is freshness. Every cup is instantly brewed in front of you, a moment before you drink it; in most cases the coffee beans are also ground immediately before brewing. Other restaurant brewing methods make anywhere from a pot to an urn at a time from pre-ground coffee, then let it sit, where it loses precious flavor and aroma to the detriment of the coffee and the advantage of the ambiance.

heart of the machine

The heart of this marvelous machine is a water tank and heating element. Water is heated to boiling inside the tank. A space is left at the top of the tank, where steam gathers. When a valve is opened below the water line, the pressure of the steam trapped at the top of the tank forces hot water out the valve and down through the coffee.

The oldest café machines and most home espresso machines work on this simple principle. It was originated by one Louis Bernard Rabaut in 1822, and first applied to a large café machine by Edward Loysel de Santais in 1843. Santais' machine wowed the Paris Exposition of 1855 by producing "two thousand cups of coffee an hour." More than likely Santais' machine brewed coffee a pot at a time. It remained for some Italians around the turn of the century to modify Santais' invention and turn it into the first modern espresso machine. They decreased the size of the strainer which held the coffee, but increased the number of valves, enabling these "rapid filter" machines to produce several single cups of coffee simultaneously, rather than a single big pot at a time.

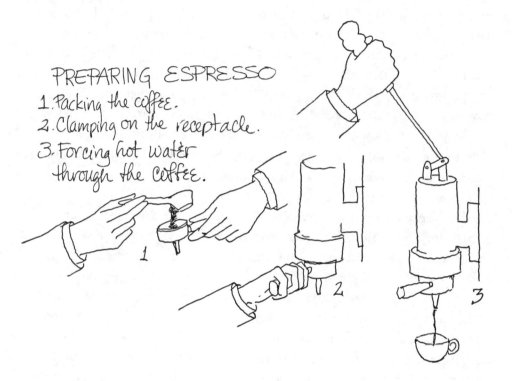

PREPARING ESPRESSO
1. Packing the coffee.
2. Clamping on the receptacle.
3. Forcing hot water
   through the coffee.

Then as now, the espresso operator packed a few teaspoons of very finely ground, dark-roast coffee into a little strainer. He clamped the strainer into a receptacle protruding from the side of the machine. When he opened the valve (or in more modern machines when he pulls a handle or pushes a button), hot water was forced through the coffee and into the cup.

The early espresso machines look like shiny steam engines pointed at the ceiling. The round water tank is set on end, and bristles with picturesque spouts, valves, and pressure gauges. These shiny, eagle-topped towers dominated the European café scene until World War II. After the war the new Italian wanted an even stronger cup of coffee to go with his Vespa, and he wanted it faster. The water tank was laid on its side, and concealed inside a

the early machines

ESPRESSO

spring powered

streamlined metal cabinet with lines like a Danish-modern jukebox. The simple valve of the old days was replaced with a spring-powered piston, which pushed the water through the coffee even harder and faster. To see how, look at the facing illustration. When the lever (A) is pulled down, the piston (B) is lifted, allowing a measured amount of hot water into the compartment (C) above the coffee (D). The spring (E) then forces the piston down, which in turn forces the water through the coffee, and allows the handle to return slowly and majestically to its original position.

hydraulic powered

In the sixties, just when pumping the handles became the dramatic trademark of espresso cafés, a third method of forcing the water through the coffee was devised. The piston is powered by water pressure, and the long handles replaced by a button. To see what the button does, return to the illustration. Note that there are two cylinders, a large one set atop a small. Inside each cylinder is a piston; the pistons are connected. The smaller cylinder and piston push hot water through the coffee (F) just as in the spring-loaded machines. But here the spring and long handle have been replaced by the larger cylinder. When the operator pushes a button, *tap* water (*not* hot water from the tank) enters the *larger* cylinder at G, forcing the larger piston (H) upwards. The large piston lifts the small piston (I). This means hot water from the tank is allowed to enter the small cylinder at J. Next a valve (K) is automatically triggered; tap water now enters the large cylinder above the piston at L, forcing the large piston down, pushing the tap water below the piston out, and forcing the hot water in the small cylinder down through the coffee and into the cup.

Technically this last is the best system of all, since hydraulic pressure is more consistent, powerful, and easily controlled than spring pressure. It is also easier on the operator's bicep, although pushing a button doesn't come close to the smooth pull on that long, shiny handle for drama and delicious flourish. The push-button machines carry the streamlined look to its extreme. Everything, even the fixture which houses the piston, is concealed inside enamel and chrome.

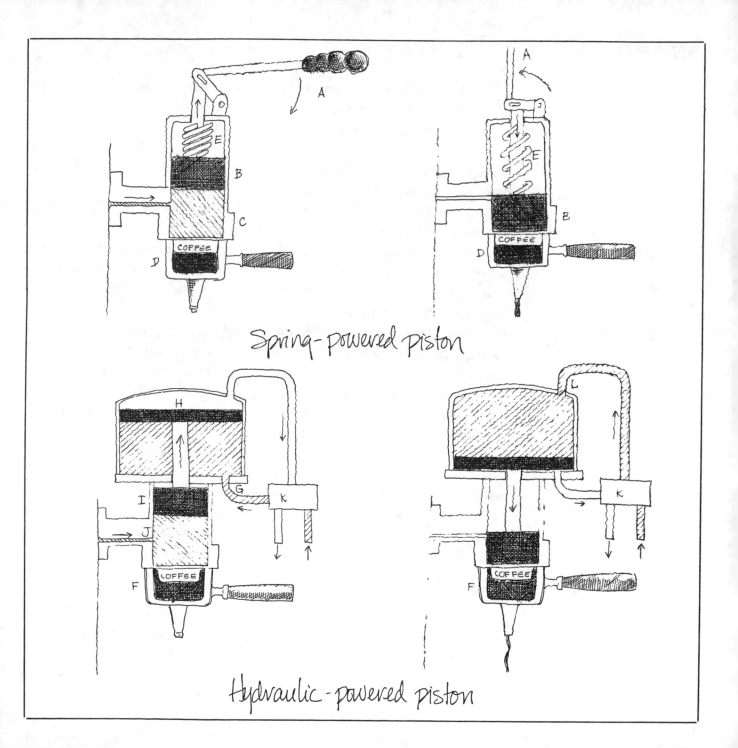

Spring-powered piston

Hydraulic-powered piston

ESPRESSO

There are signs of reaction to such austerity, however. In some cases North American cafés are buying the older machines with handles, machines which the Italians have discarded for the new push-button models. (This development is an amusing reversal of the post-World War II days when European countries bought used machinery from the United States.) And at least one importer has been doctoring up the new push-button machines with a lot of useless but delicious gimcrackery reminiscent of the old days:

delicious gimcrackery

copper and brass tubes, eagles, dials, and whatnot. These fanciful machines are selling much more rapidly than the cheaper modern-look machines, a fact which bears out my feeling that North Americans want drama as well as good coffee, and the Italians blew it for us romantic provincials when they introduced the push-button machine.

With the long pull on the shiny handle gone the way of the running board, one of the best remaining schticks left to the espresso operator is heating and foaming the milk. Espresso is a strong, concentrated coffee, and in accordance with European tradition, many of the drinks in the espresso cuisine combine it with large quantities of milk. If the milk were not heated, it would instantly cool the coffee. Early in the history of the espresso machine someone realized that the steam collected in the top of the tank could be used to heat milk as well as provide pressure for coffee making. A valve with a long nozzle was let into the upper part of the tank where the steam gathers. When the valve is opened by unscrewing a knob, the compressed steam comes hissing out of the end of the nozzle. Cold milk is poured into a pitcher; the espresso operator shoves the nozzle into the milk and opens the valve. The compressed steam shoots out through the milk, both heating it and raising an attractive head of froth or foam.

steamed milk

Café patrons soon discovered that steamed, foamed milk both tastes and looks better than milk heated in the ordinary way, and it became an important part of espresso cuisine. The white head of foam is decorative, can be garnished with a dash of cocoa or cinnamon, prevents a skin from forming on the surface of the milk, and insulates the hot coffee.

It is difficult to say how much of the success of the espresso machine is owing to its scientifically impeccable approach to coffee making, or its drama and novelty, but given European tastes it certainly does put out a remarkable cup of coffee: absolutely freshly ground and freshly brewed, and so quickly brewed that, as an Italian friend of mine says, you get only the *heart* of the coffee.

Nevertheless, many a coffee lover facing a cup of espresso for the first time may take one swallow, and either finish it stoically or hide the little cup behind his napkin. His distaste is understandable: This impeccable brewing system is designed to make a cup of coffee in the southern European or Latin American tradition, rather than the northern European or North American. Good espresso is rich, heavy-bodied, almost syrupy, and has the characteristic bittersweet bite of dark-roasted coffee. Its sharp flavor and heavy body make it an ideal coffee to be drunk with milk and sugar, but hardly the sort of beverage to be drunk unsweetened, or in large quantities.

in the southern European tradition

Most espresso drinkers outside Italy prefer a cappuccino, a drink made of about one-third espresso and two-thirds hot milk and foam. The milk dilutes and mellows the strong, sharp coffee. With a home espresso machine, one can of course use a lighter-roasted coffee and come out with a drink with the same richness as café espresso, but without the dark-roasted tang.

Southern Europeans have drunk strong, sharply-flavored coffee in small cups or mixed with hot milk for generations. Consequently, most of the drinks in the espresso cuisine are not original with the machine; rather, the machine brought them from promise to perfection. Here are some of the most popular:

Espresso A single demitasse of espresso coffee, black, usually drunk with sugar. Can be flavored with a drop or two of almond or tangerine extract.

espresso drinks

Espresso Romano A demitasse of espresso served with a twist or a thin slice of lemon on the side.

Double or Doppio A full six-ounce cup of straight espresso. To be drunk

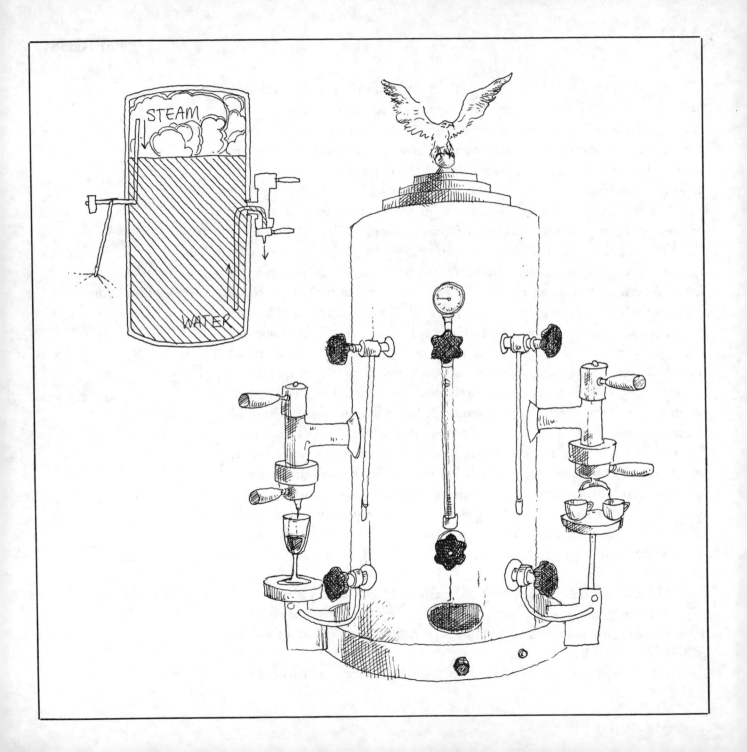

STEAM

WATER

only by veteran espresso bibbers, early in the morning, before a 12-hour work day and a long evening.

Cappuccino (French: *café crème*) About one-third espresso, one-third hot milk, topped with one-third foam, in a heavy cup. Like the others, usually drunk with sugar.

Caffè Latte (French: *café au lait;* Spanish: *café con leche*) One or two shots of espresso, and three times as much foamed milk, in a big bowl or wide-mouthed glass. This is the favored breakfast drink of southern Europeans. Caffè latte has a greater proportion of milk to coffee than a cappuccino, and tastes weaker and milkier. Strictly speaking, the milk and coffee should be poured simultaneously, one from either side of the bowl. The hot milk and coffee are often served separately in Europe.

Espresso Macchiato A demitasse of espresso "marked" ("macchiato") with a small quantity of hot, foamed milk.

Latte Macchiato A glass half-filled with hot, foamed milk, into which a demitasse of espresso is slowly dribbled. The coffee will color the milk in faint, graduated layers, darker at the top shading to light at the bottom, all contrasting to the layer of pure white foam at the top.

Mocha: Not to be confused with Mocha-Java, a traditional American-roasted blend of Mocha and Java coffees. A "mocha" to an espresso aficionado is about one-third espresso, one-third strong, unsweetened hot chocolate, and one-third steamed milk. The milk goes in last, and the whole thing is usually served in a mug. Voltaire is said to have consumed 40 cups of mocha a day at the Café Procope.

Some cafés garnish the foam of the cappuccino and caffè latte with a dash of unsweetened cocoa, which adds the subtle perfume of chocolate to the drink. Others use cinnamon, which I don't approve of; I find it too distinctive a flavor and out of harmony with the dark tones of the coffee. Straight espresso is delicious with whipped cream *(con panna),* but topping a good, foamy cappuccino with whipped cream is as pointless as putting catsup on spaghetti.

garnishing the foam

ESPRESSO

Unfortunately, few North American coffee drinkers have an opportunity to experience the extraordinary perfume of the true espresso coffee. Most of the alleged *cappuccini* I've tasted outside the best cafés of San Francisco or New York resemble a somewhat superior version of instant coffee and hot hilk. Sometimes café owners load a lot of canned whipped cream and cinnamon on top in an apparent effort to romanticize the grim reality underneath. The act of cappuccino, as practiced in the espresso bars of Italy, is a gesture of pure truth, transcendent. Tasting one makes me want to start praising God, or at least applauding vigorously.

The two principal mistakes I've observed being committed by would-be espresso purveyors are using a pre-ground coffee and letting too much water run through the grounds. The purpose of the espresso system is to produce an absolutely fresh cup of coffee, custom brewed on demand. Using a pre-ground, canned coffee, rather than fresh-ground coffee from the matched grinders made to accompany the big machines, defeats this system at its source. And allowing too much water to flow through even fresh-ground coffee will produce a thin, bitter cup. The espresso system is so efficient that the goodness is extracted from the ground coffee almost immediately, producing, as I've said, a small amount of intense brew, usually no more than an ounce per serving. If you want more quantity in your cup, then you should drink another style of coffee or order a cappuccino, which mixes the small amount of intense coffee with two or three times as much milk.

If you *have* tasted a really fine espresso or cappuccino, however, and you want more, you may want to cut out the restaurateurs and make your own. In this case, your first step should be deciding what you like about it. For instance, if you like the pungent *flavor* of the espresso and are indifferent to the rich texture of the coffee itself, or the effect of foamed milk, then you may be just as happy with dark-roasted coffee, made in the ordinary way. Start with half a pound of the darkest roast in the store, ground for your regular coffee maker.

If it turns out that you like the rich, creamy *texture* of straight espresso, or if you simply want a strong European-style coffee for brandy and whiskey drinks, you can purchase one of the many good, inexpensive espresso machines *without steam valves,* described below. Make sure you read my instructions on making espresso, however, since used unknowledgeably these machines can make very bad coffee.

If you like steamed milk with your espresso, then prepare to spend a minimum of $50 on a machine with an attachment for steaming milk. And if you want a flashy machine for entertaining and display at the dinner table, then prepare to pay even more. Before I describe the range of machines available in each category, I had better brief you on what you're in for.

First the coffee. The standard espresso roast, also called Italian and sometimes French, is a good place to start. But remember that you can make any coffee in your espresso maker, so long as it is properly ground. You may want a coffee darker than espresso roast, or lighter. No matter what coffee you choose, you will always come out with the rich texture and heavy body of espresso. But only with the darker roasts will you come out with the sharp tang of true café espresso. In general, use as much coffee as is needed to fill the coffee receptacle of your machine. If in doubt, use two level tablespoons of finely ground coffee for every demitasse of espresso.

There are two tricks to making good home espresso. First, you need to grind your coffee just fine enough, and tamp it down in the receptacle just hard enough, so the water is forced through the coffee *slowly*. Second, you need to stop the brewing process at just the correct moment. To return to the first point: If the coffee is ground finely enough and tamped down firmly enough, and you keep the heat high enough, you'll come out with a dark, rich, sweet brew, topped with the delicate brown foam which marks your espresso as the real stuff. If the coffee is ground too coarsely or not packed down hard enough, the water will come gushing through, and you'll end up with watery, bitter stuff that will send you and your guests back to the percolator. If the coffee is ground *too* finely or packed *too* tightly, nothing at all may happen until the trapped steam pops the safety valve and an explosive hiss fills your kitchen, indicating you have quite literally blown it by not allowing *any* water to penetrate the coffee.

best grind

The best grind is very fine, gritty, but *not* a dusty powder. If you look at it from a foot away you should be barely able to distinguish particles. If you rub some between your fingers, it should feel gritty. Most canned espresso coffees, like Medaglia D'Oro or Motta, are ground much too coarsely. Your best bet as usual is your own grinder, but if you're really lazy or cheap try some of the less widely distributed canned espressos: Aromatic Best Caffe, Café Gaviña in the Los Angeles area, and Café Bustelo on the East Coast. If you have whole beans ground at the store, ask for "very fine grind, for an espresso machine."

Fill the receptacle to the brim with coffee, then *lightly* and *evenly* tamp it down. If you fear the grind is too coarse, tamp heavily; if too fine, tamp lightly. If your grind is fine enough, you should put your pot on a medium to high heat in order to build sufficient steam pressure to force the water through the barrier of fine-grained coffee. If the coffee gushes, rather than dribbles, out, you must compensate by reducing the heat, or better yet, by using a finer grind coffee.

the right timing

The richest espresso comes out right at the beginning; as brewing continues it becomes progressively thinner and more bitter. This is because the espresso brewing system is so efficient it removes almost all the flavorful elements from the coffee right at the start, leaving nothing but harsh chemicals for last. So the second trick is to remove the pot from the heat at the proper moment, *before* the coffee starts gushing out weak and thin. This is not as difficult as it sounds; the first time you make coffee in your espresso pot keep the cover off and watch the coffee come out. The first few spurts will be dark and syrupy. Soon a dark, but somewhat lighter-bodied stuff will begin running out steadily. When the coffee starts coming out so thin you can see through it, or when it starts gushing and sputtering rather than running out, you've gone too far. At any rate, with some practice and observation, you should be able to time it all correctly. Brew only as much coffee as you will actually serve, since the less you brew the richer and sweeter it will be.

A warning: If you leave the pot on the heat without water in the reservoir, you will reduce the gaskets in the joints of the pot to bubbling doughnuts of rubber. And a note about the size of pot you buy: A "six-cup" espresso machine will usually make only about *three demitasse* cups of good espresso. A "nine-cup" will make only four or five. So if in doubt, buy a larger pot than you think you need.

There are three steps to making an espresso drink with foamed milk. First, make the coffee, second, foam the milk, and third, combine the two. Never foam the coffee and the milk together; such slipshod democracy would stale the fresh coffee and ruin the eye-pleasing contrast between the white foam and dark coffee.

So assume the coffee is made. You can either foam the milk in the cups before you add the coffee, or in a separate pitcher. Either way, fill the cup or container about halfway with cold milk (the colder the better; hot milk will not foam). The steam jet is a little pipe which protrudes from the top or side of your machine, with a screw knob for opening or closing it. When one is making coffee, one normally keeps this valve screwed closed, to maintain pressure. On the tip of the steam jet are two to four little holes, which project steam downward and diagonally, in little jets. Open the steam valve just a crack before you insert the nozzle into the pitcher, to prevent milk from being sucked back up into the tube.

Heating the milk is easy; getting a head of foam is a little trickier, and like centering the clay on a potter's wheel, difficult to explain in words. First thrust the nozzle deeply into the milk. Then open the valve a couple of turns, and close it again gradually until you get a strong, but not explosive, hiss of steam. Now lower the milk container until the steam starts bubbling or hissing just below the surface of the milk. If you have the nozzle too

getting it to foam

131

STEAMING MILK
1. Inserting the steam jet and opening the valve.
2. Foaming the milk. 3. Heating the milk.

deeply into the milk there will be no hiss or bubble; if you have it too shallow it will spray milk all over the kitchen. If you have it just right, a gratifying head of foam will begin rising from the surface of the milk.

After you have a good head of foam, feel the sides of the container to see if the milk is hot enough. If not, lower the nozzle to the bottom of the container and keep it there until the sides heat up. Never boil the milk, and *always foam the milk first*, before you heat it, since cold milk foams best.

If you get a few big bubbles, rather than the many tiny ones which go to make up a strong, stable head of foam, either knock the bottom of the pitcher on the counter or let it sit for a couple of minutes before you combine the milk with the coffee. If the jet of steam is too weak to really churn the milk around, raise the heat and make certain no pressure is escaping through the coffee valve.

always foam first

Small home espresso machines all work on the same principle: There is a water reservoir at the bottom, a receptacle to receive the brewed coffee above or to the side of the reservoir, and between them a receptacle for the ground coffee. Steam pressure in the water reservoir forces the boiling water up through the ground coffee, and it comes out espresso.

Besides price, the two criteria for choosing a pot are the material used for the part which receives the brewed coffee, and design. The most widely distributed machine is the Moka Express ($14 to $35). Since it is made entirely of cast aluminum, I do not recommend it. Aluminum can impart a slight metallic taste to the drink. and conducts heat so efficiently it may overheat the freshly brewed coffee and totally spoil the flavor. Other manufacturers get around this problem with stainless steel (Jata, around $35; the attractive "Carmencita Lavazza" at $60; and also at $60 the snazzy "Allesi Caffetteria Espresso," another resident in the Design Collection of the Museum of Modern Art). Even better are the pots with ceramic tops. The water boils in an aluminum base and the coffee ends up in a ceramic receptacle. In some the ceramic part lifts off the base and can be carried to the table separately. There are several of these pots available, ranging in look from the flowery English to the austerely Italian, and in price from $30 to about $50. The Vesuviana ($25 to $35; $65 with built-in electric element) is in a class by itself, all aluminum but with a fine old-fashioned Italian caffè air to it. The receptacle for the ground coffee clamps on as it does on the big machines.

If you already have a good espresso machine without an attachment for steaming milk, or simply want to top regular coffee with steamed milk, a good buy would be the Cappuccin-Olà (the distributer pronounces it "olay") milk steamer. It sells for around $50, and is safe, efficient, and well made. You can foam large amounts of milk, plus heat apple cider, chocolate, buttered rum, and anything else you want hot but not boiled. It actually functions as an all-around kitchen aid, and would make anyone happy who likes to entertain with hot drinks. The matching hot plate sells for around

$25. Vesubio makes a sturdy little steamer with a smaller capacity ("La Steam") for around $50, although I've seen it on sale for considerably less.

with steam attachment

If you don't have a satisfactory espresso maker, you will want to buy one that also steams milk. These all-purpose machines have the added advantage of providing some means for cutting off the flow of brewed coffee without taking the pot off the heat, a virtue in a brewing system in which timing is so important. The two most widely available machines that combine espresso making and milk steaming are the Vesubio and the Via Veneto. Both sell for between $70 and $100 and are nearly identical in appearance: a keg-like water reservoir topped with two tubes. The espresso comes out of one tube and the steam out of the other; both are controlled by screw valves. Another possibility, the Atomic Espresso, sells for anywhere from $50 to $100, and looks like a cross between a mushroom cloud and an overstuffed chair. It will make excellent cappuccino, but requires close attention. One design flaw is the clumsy, makeshift arrangement for cutting off the flow of brewing coffee: You stick a brass rod into a hole in the coffee receptacle, and more often than not coffee continues to sputter out around the brass rod. The second problem is the decanter for the brewed coffee, which is made of aluminum and thus may overheat and taint the fresh-brewed espresso. If you do buy the Atomic, replace the aluminum decanter with something ceramic.

at the table

The Via Veneto also comes with a hotplate/warmer and matching carafe, which enables you to make your *cappuccini* at the table. This version is called a "Signor Cappuccino I" ($140 to $160) or "Signor Cappuccino II" ($120 to $140). There doesn't seem to be much difference between the two except for external design and price. I would pass them both up and buy the stove-top model because you can control the heat for better steam pressure and thicker espresso. Two other units with both milk steamer and built-in heating unit are the Pronto Caffè ($90), a flimsy, unstable little machine, mostly plastic and with a small water capacity, and the Café Salton, ($175), a better looking but still flimsy machine that makes filter coffee as well as

Vesuviana

CERAMIC-TOP POT

Moka Express

BREWED COFFEE

GROUND COFFEE

WATER RESERVOIR

espresso and steamed milk. The espresso takes a while; 11 minutes to the pot. The steamer will heat milk, but is useless for raising a head of foam, since there's a little valve on the end of the steam tube which can only be opened by shoving it against the bottom of the milk container. If you've read my instructions for frothing milk, you know that to raise a proper foamy head you need to keep the live steam at the *surface* of the milk, not at the bottom.

All in all, these mid-priced cappuccino makers are a sad lot; one wonders if the designers were tea drinkers. My recommendation is the stove-top Via Veneto. It's sturdy, simple, and if you're careful and follow my instructions, will make an excellent cappuccino.

LARGER HOME MACHINES

For real perfectionists, as well as dedicated show-offs, there are miniature versions of the café giants. All are self-contained, with their own built-in heating element. As in the big machines, the ground coffee is held in a small receptacle that clamps onto the larger unit, enabling one to make a cup or two at a time without emptying, cleaning, and refilling the entire machine. Most also have some arrangement to intensify the pressure used to force the water through the ground coffee, making for a richer, foamier espresso.

These larger home machines fall into two groups: the athletic and the automatic. In the athletic, a handle protrudes from the front of the machine, making it look much like the old-fashioned café models. The handle acts as a lever. You lean on it, forcing a measured quantity of water directly down through the coffee. With the automatic machines you just push a button and out comes espresso. In some cases the button simply opens a valve and ordinary steam pressure forces the water through the coffee, just as in the smaller machines; in others the button activates a mechanical pump that gives the hot water an extra boost.

Some notes and recommendations:

recommendations   *Krups Gaggia* (also *Baby Gaggia;* $500) A consistently praised push-button machine with several top-of-the-line features. Rather than gradually building

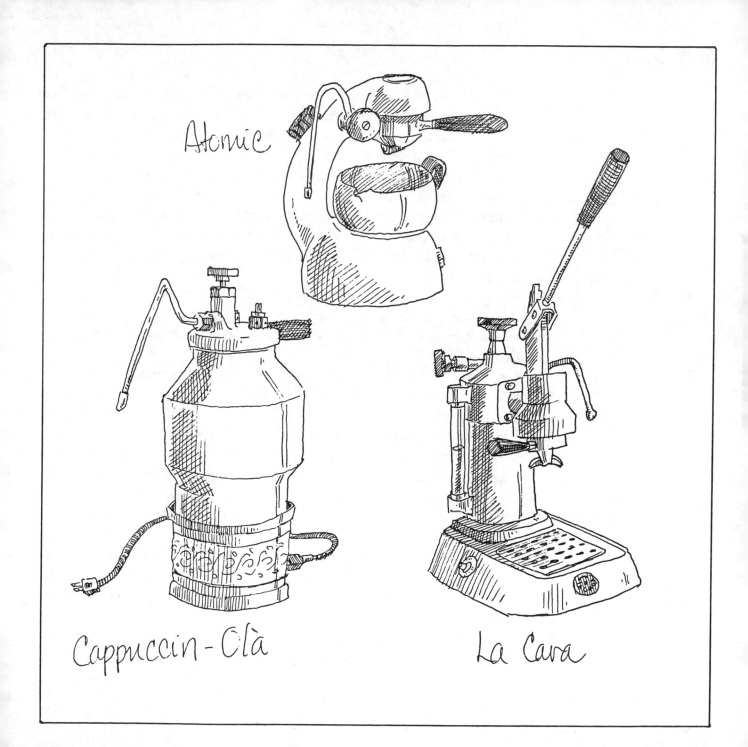

Atomic

Cappuccin-Clà

La Cava

pressure in an entire tank of water, the Gaggia heats two cups at a time in a smaller reservoir. Consequently it has a faster start-up time (two minutes for the first two cups; 45 seconds for subsequent servings). Most of the larger home machines must be cooled to be refilled and turned upside down to be drained. In the Gaggia the main water reservoir can be refilled, and even lifted out and drained while the machine is in operation. The Gaggia also comes with four 2-cup receptacles for ground coffee, enabling one to load up for company in advance. It is a good-looking machine, solidly constructed of enameled cast iron. Like virtually all of these larger machines, it makes excellent espresso.

Olympia *Olympia Maxi-Matic* ($450) Another widely praised push-button machine. Same water capacity as the Gaggia (two quarts); slower to heat to operating temperature (six minutes), but a bit faster on repeats. Must be turned upside down to drain.

Olympia Cremina ($300) A version of the Maxi-Matic with a lever-action handle rather than push-button pump. I prefer the lever mechanism to the pump; it gives you better control over the brewing operation, is simpler and less liable to malfunction, and makes for a cheaper machine. The Cremina has the largest water capacity (four quarts) of the machines noted here; it takes 6½ minutes to reach operating temperature, however, must be cooled for refilling, and the entire machine must be inverted to drain.

Micro Cimbali *Micro Cimbali* ($450) A sturdy machine with lever handle; the water tank is partly exposed, giving the machine a more traditional look than the boxier models listed so far. Smaller water capacity (1½ quarts) and slower to warm up (ten minutes) than most of the others. The Micro Cimbali can be partially drained without turning the entire machine over, but the last few ounces of water can only be removed by inverting.

Rowoco *Rowoco Espresso—Cappuccino* ($300) Another push-button model; it does not appear to be as sturdy, nor is it as flashy looking, as the larger home machines listed so far; it also has a much smaller water capacity (five cups).

It has a fast warm-up, however (two minutes), and the water reservoir is removable, making draining and refilling simple.

La Pavoni Europiccola ($180) The least expensive and most widely distributed of the larger home machines. Sturdy, with lever action and an endearing old-fashioned look reminiscent of the eagle-topped towers of pre-World War II days. Technically it has its problems, however; it makes good espresso but the steam is not as explosive and virile as one might wish. It has a very small capacity (three cups) and is relatively slow to warm up (seven minutes). Used carefully, however, the Europiccola will make an excellent cappuccino. *La Pavoni*

La Cara ($200) A somewhat larger version of the Europiccola, with somewhat better steam pressure; available only from Thomas Cara in San Francisco. Can be hooked up directly to your plumbing system. *La Cara*

Riviera ($500) Same size and features as the La Cara, but fancier looking, in the antique caffè mode. *Riviera*

My recommendations: Olympia Cremina first; Krups Gaggia if you prefer an automatic model. For the price La Cara is excellent. If you decide to go all the way with your espresso habit and buy one of the larger machines, be sure to shop before you buy; prices for the same machine vary greatly from store to store. Have the salesperson demonstrate the machine, and make certain you know how to operate it.

If these larger machines don't make a good enough cappuccino for you, then you had better either open a café, or do as the French used to and spend your life in one, sipping café crème and exploring *les faits du jour.*

ARAB COFFEE SHOP

8 SERVING IT
The social sacrament; from Arabian coffee ceremony to thermos jug

R ITUAL HAS a bad name in the contemporary world; it invokes visions of incense, dark places, and vaguely enslaving mumbo jumbo. In matters of food and drink it connotes snobbishness, an overemphasis on form and manners at the expense of genuine satisfaction. Nevertheless, no matter how modishly alienated or culturally rootless, everyone lives his life profoundly committed to ritual. Construction workers drinking beer on Friday afternoon, middle-class couples coming home to their martinis on the rocks, counter-culturites sitting on the floor rolling joints, are all performing rituals which celebrate their solidarity with others, and make them feel expansive and secure.

rituals

Ritual often chooses for its vehicle consciousness-altering substances like alcohol, marijuana, or coffee. Primitive cultures often assume a bit of god resides in these substances, because through them we are separated for a moment from the ordinariness of things, and somehow seize our own reality more clearly. This is why so many rituals are, besides a gesture of hospitality and reassurance, a celebration of a break in routine, a moment when the human drive to survival lets up, and we simply *are,* together. This last is to me the real meaning of the coffee break, the coffee klatsch, the cocktail hour, the beer bust, and after-dinner coffee. Coffee and spirits are pre-eminently the sacramental drugs of our culture, though we may soon add marijuana to the list.

Often the reason we call one person more "civilized" than another is because he has mastered the rituals of his culture with more assurance and finesse than others. I don't mean this snobbishly; Paul Newman can be said to know how to open a can of beer better than anyone living, because opening a can of beer is more than a practical matter of getting at what's inside. Done right it makes one a man in the full-on North American sense; done wrong it makes one an outcast or object of pity. The same may be said in other circles for opening a wine bottle or rolling a joint.

tea ceremony

In some cultures the ritual aspects of drinking tea or coffee, or smoking tobacco, are given a semi-religious status. The most famous of such rituals is the Japanese tea ceremony, in which a strong powdered green tea is whipped in an ancient bowl to form a rich frothy drink, which is then ceremonially passed, in total silence, from one participant to the next. The tea ceremony is quite consciously structured as a sort of communal meditation, a few minutes devoted to contemplating the presence of eternity in the moment. Doubtless the caffeine in the tea aids in such psychic enterprise.

Allowed to degenerate, however, such rituals simply become excuses to display our ancient tea bowls, latest martini pitcher, or our groovy water pipe from Nepal. A Swedish friend of mine once told me she felt the coffee klatsch was less a communion of friends than a chance for the hostess to show off her baking. This is the sort of thing that gives ritual a bad name.

witchcraft and fertility

Coffee from the beginning has been one of humanity's sacramental substances. In Africa, for instance, it is used in witchcraft and fertility rites. Fredrick Wellman, in *Coffee: Botany, Cultivation, and Utilization*, describes an African blood brother ceremony in which "blood of the two pledging parties is mixed and put between the twin seeds of a coffee fruit and the whole swallowed."

Coffee in its hot, black, modern form was first used as a medicine, next as an aid to prayer and meditation by Arabian monastics, much as green tea is used by Zen monks in Japan to celebrate and fortify. Pilgrims to Mecca then carried coffee all over the Moslem world, and it became secularized, but the religious association remained. Some Christians were at first wont to brand coffee as "that blacke bitter invention of Satan," as opposed to good Christian wine, but the 16th century Pope Clement VIII is said to have sampled the stuff, and declaring it was too good to let the Moslems have it all, gave it his official blessing.

With the Moslems, however, particularly with the Arabs, coffee has maintained its religious connotation, and the ritual aspects apparently remain refined and conscious. There is, in fact, an Arabian coffee ceremony, which, had American intellectuals turned to Arabia rather than to Japan for a modern philosophy of art, might rival the tea ceremony in influence. It is very similar, and properly performed, doubtlessly as beautiful.

coffee ceremony

Ritual is further wrapped up in the smell and taste of coffee itself. Certain smells, flavors, movements, sounds combine to symbolize *coffee* and suggest a mood of well-being in an entire nation. This, I'm convinced, is the reason for the persistence of the pumping percolator in American culture: To an American it *sounds* and *smells* like coffee, and makes him feel good before he even lifts a cup.

Other cultures have similarly arbitrary associations: To the Middle Easterner the foam that gathers in the pot when he cooks his coffee is an indispensable part of the drink, not because it tastes good, but because it symbolizes the meditative glow of *coffee*. Italian and other hard-core espresso aficionados put a similar, if somewhat less ceremonial, emphasis on foam. An Italian will not take a cup of espresso seriously if it isn't topped with a thin layer of what to a filter coffee drinker probably looks like brown scum; the foam is what marks it as the *real stuff*. A similar satisfaction resides in the foamy milk that tops drinks like caffè latte or cappuccino. The foam has no flavor, but a cappuccino is not a cappuccino without it.

foam

SERVING IT

Ritual is what gives validity to the variety of cups, pots, and paraphernalia human beings have developed to simply transport coffee from the pot to the belly. There are of course practical matters involved, notably keeping the coffee hot on the way, but most variations are refinements which solely answer the very real need for the satisfaction of ritual. Of course, if you buy those Italian demitasse cups or the sterling serving pot, not because they make your spirit glow, but because you think it might impress the folks with your continental flair, then you're a snob, and you'd better see your local existentialist for authenticity lessons.

keeping it hot

Again, the only practical contribution serving paraphernalia can make to our coffee-drinking pleasure is keeping the stuff hot. Obviously you can do this two ways: provide a heat source, or keep the coffee in a container which retains heat. A continuing heat source is virtually indispensible with Melitta, Chemex, and other filter brewers, since the brewing process takes so long. Most filter brewers can't be put directly on the burner, and you would risk boiling or overheating your coffee anyhow; you need to buffer the heat with either a heat-reducing pad or a hot water bath. If you are not concerned with esthetics you can simply immerse the bottom part of your filter coffee maker in a pot of hot water. Chemex makes an an attractive copper utensil for this purpose for around $15. David Douglass offers a "heat reducing stand" for around $4, Chemex a heat-reducing grid, and you can usually find a Mouli Radiant Heat Plate in any cooking-gear shop for about $3.

If you want to keep your filter coffee warm at the table, you can choose between an adjustable electric warmer like the Salton Hotray, a candle warmer, or a warmer especially made for filter coffee makers, like the Melitta ($16) or Chemex ($22).

covered pots

Covered pots for serving coffee have been in vogue since the Arabs started drinking it. At import stores you can still find the traditional Arabian serving pot, with its "S" shaped spout, Aladdin's lamp pedestal and pointed cover. You can also occasionally find an *ibrik,* or Middle Eastern coffee maker, with an embossed cover for keeping the coffee hot between servings.

The changes in English coffee-pot design are fascinating. On one hand stands the severe, straight-sided pewter pot of the 17th century, which suggests a Puritan in his stiff collar; on the other, the silver coffee pots of the Romantic revival, which take the original Arabian design and make it seethe with enough squiggles and flourishes to fulfill the most ardent fantasies of a romantic nobleman should he glance up from the latest gothic fiction to contemplate the imitation oriental splendor of his sitting room reflected in the shimmering arabesques of his coffee pot.

Ever since, coffee-server design has wobbled between these two extremes. Today the coffee pot and matching sugar dish and creamer have gone out of fashion, but will doubtless return along with the pillbox hat and the antimacassar. More widely available today is the continental-style coffee server. It is smaller than the English-style pot, and has a straight handle protruding from the body of the pot like an arrow sticking out of a cowboy. The French often serve the coffee part of café au lait in a pot of this kind, and put the hot milk in another, small, open-topped pitcher. You're sup-

continental-style server

145

posed to pick up the coffee in one hand and the milk in another, and pour both into the bowl simultaneously, in one smooth gesture. The straight handle, which points toward you and rolls in your hand as you pour, makes this important operation easier to manage with proper continental flair. I've seen these pots in copper for around $17.

serving thermos The space-age contribution to coffee serving is the thermos; it works like the old thermos jug, but has a bit more class. The serving thermos keeps coffee hot for hours, and though the aroma goes quickly, the flavor holds well. A family which eats breakfast in shifts, or anyone who likes to keep his coffee hot for an hour or **two** or more, might want to purchase a serving thermos. It is much easier on flavor than reheating. The cheapest, like the Swedish Decape ($15) and Hammarplast ($18), are all plastic and have a bright, aggressive contemporary chic. Stainless steel models, also with a contemporary look, sell for $20 to $25, and traditional-look brass or silver plate for $60 and up.

mugs and cups Coffee is probably best served in heavy ceramic mugs or cups which have been warmed first with a little hot water. There are many directions to take: fancy china, folksy hand-thrown earthenware, cheaper Japanese mugs which look hand-thrown, and heavy, classic mugs and cups from restaurant-supply stores. I like the restaurant-supply stuff myself; it looks solid, feels authentic, reflects the hearty democratic tradition of coffee, and bounces when you drop it on the average formica counter.

demitasse Straight espresso, after-dinner coffees brewed double-strength, and Middle Eastern coffees are traditionally served in a half-size, or demitasse cup. There seems to be something perfectly appropriate to drinking such intense, perfumy stuff out of small cups rather than from the usual ingratiatingly generous mugs and cups. You should have the small demitasse spoons to go with the cups; an ordinary spoon looks like a shovel next to a demitasse cup. You can save considerable money on such gear at a restaurant-supply store. A set of stainless-steel demitasse spoons, for instance, will cost one-tenth what they will anywhere else, and if they don't look good enough to you,

you probably have enough money to buy sterling. Nearly every espresso specialty—cappuccino, mocha, caffè latte—has its preferred style of cup, mug, or glass; I introduce them along with the drinks in Chapter 7.

German and Scandinavian tradition calls for paper-thin porcelain cups, to go with the water-thin coffee served at the traditional *Kaffeeklatsch*. Andres Uribe, in his book *Brown Gold*, claims the ladies at the original German *Kaffeeklatschen* called their coffee *Blumechenkaffee*, "flower-coffee," after the little painted flowers which their thin, tea-like beverage permitted them to see all too clearly at the bottom of their Dresden cups.

When I was a teenager in the Midwest circa 1955, drinking your coffee any other way than black made your manhood suspect, or your dates wonder whether you were the kind of woman who ate two-pound boxes of chocolate while reading movie magazines. People would leer patronizingly at you, and tell you that you couldn't possibly like coffee that much if you had to add cream and sugar to it. I assume they didn't like beef, since most of them ate it cooked and seasoned. Perhaps the North American preference for thin, black coffee goes along with an equivalent love of characterless white wines, dry martinis, and lager beer. It's as though to admit to liking sweet, heavy drinks is tantamount to admitting some unpardonable weakness, like a penchant for Perry Como or cocker spaniels.

MILK AND SUGAR
the great debate

unpardonable weakness

One reason for the prejudice in the United States against milk in coffee may be the prevailing style of the coffee: If you add *anything* to the average cup of thin, under-flavored stuff they serve in most restaurants, you eliminate what little there was to taste in the first place. On the other hand, dark-roasted European-style coffees, and all the great rich, full-bodied coffees of the world, brewed correctly, will carry their flavor intact through nearly any amount of milk. Too much milk, of course, will cool the coffee, unless you heat it, or better yet, steam it the way European-style cafés do. Anyone who enjoys milk in his coffee might consider purchasing a milk steamer like the one described in Chapter 7.

9 CAFFEINE
The caffeine controversy
and decaffeinated coffees

WHEN SIR WILLIAM HARVEY, the 17th-century physician credited with discovering the circulation of the blood, was on his death bed, he allegedly called his lawyer to his side and held up a coffee bean. "This little Fruit," he whispered, eyes doubtless still bright from his morning cup, "is the source of happiness and wit!" Sir William then bequeathed his entire supply of coffee, 56 pounds, to the London College of Physicians, directing them to commemorate the day of his death every month with a morning round of coffee.

To some of a puritan or suspicious nature, this anecdote may strike a sinister note. Did Sir William die young? How *much* coffee did he drink, and did he have any enemies in the College of Physicians?

a sinister note

Paradox runs through the entire history of coffee. It began as medicine, and graduated to simultaneous roles as panacea and poison. Early in its history, for instance, coffee was adopted by Arabian dervishes to fortify their religious meditation. Yet no more than 50 years later, in Mecca, it was the subject of vehement religious persecutions on grounds it encouraged mirth and chess-playing among the faithful. Religion still can't make up its mind about coffee; Mormons and some fundamentalists reject it, while most

CAFFEINE

Moslems and many Christians consider it a sober and wholesome alternative to wine and spirits.

In the 17th century, when religion gave way to science and priests to doctors, the debate continued. One physician claimed coffee relieved dropsy, gravel, gout, migraine, hypochondria, and cured scurvy outright, while another declared that drunk with milk, it caused leprosy. "The lovers of coffee used the physicians very ill when they met together," says one detached French observer, "and the physicians on their side threatened the coffee drinkers with all sorts of diseases."

an unsettling accusation

One of the most unsettling accusations leveled against coffee came in a tale by a 17th-century German traveler, Adam Oelshlager, in his *Relation of a Voyage to Muscovie, Tartary, and Persia.* The story concerns the king of Persia, who "had become so habituated to the use of coffee that he took a dislike for women." One day the queen saw a stallion being emasculated; upon asking the reason she was told the animal was too spirited, and was being gelded to tame it. Whereupon the queen suggested a simpler solution would be to feed it coffee every morning. This story, when introduced into southern France, was said to have virtually ruined the coffee trade there for 50 years. On the other hand, a tale from a Persian saga reports that after the prophet Mohammed had his first cup of coffee (delivered by the angel Gabriel), he "felt able to unseat forty horsemen and possess fifty women."

aphrodisiac

I leave the relationship between coffee and potency to my readers (experiment, experiment!), but I can't help but note that capitalism's latest venture into sexual enlightenment, an over-the-counter aphrodisiac or "sexual stimulation tablet," contains 100 milligrams of caffeine, along with ginseng powder and vitamin E (which ingredients, however healthful, have doubtless considerable less effect than the caffeine on the matter immediately in hand).

It was in England of the 17th century that coffee's career as medicine reached its apex, and possibly, nadir. The most extravagant claims were launched for its medicinal value, and the most extraordinary accusations leveled against it. One Englishman named Walter Rumsey invented an "electuary" of coffee, to be taken internally with the aid of an instrument called a "provang." The "electuary" was prescribed for intestinal disorders and hysteria. First one prepared the electuary, which consisted of heated butter, salad oil, honey, and ground coffee. Next one introduced the provang, a thin bone rod about a yard long with a little button on the end, into the intestinal tract by way of the rectum, and manipulated it vigorously. Thirdly, one swallowed the electuary, and concluded the treatment with a second energetic application of the provang. I feel that it was at this point in history that tea began to replace coffee as England's favored beverage.

a thin bone rod

Out of all this confusion and debate came the world's first scientific analysis of coffee. In 1685, Dr. Sylvestre Dufour described the chemical constituents of coffee with some accuracy, and apparently through numerous experiments on human beings, came to the same conclusion virtually every other researcher has come to since: Some people can drink coffee comfortably and some can't. Dufour even found a few who slept better after drinking coffee than before, probably because, in Dufour's words, the coffee "relieved their disquiet, and removed their feeling of anxiety."

Dufour also helped the critics of coffee identify for the first time their true enemy: the odorless, bitter alkaloid caffeine. The average cup of American-style coffee contains about 100 milligrams of caffeine; a demitasse of espresso may contain up to twice as much. The average cup of tea contains about 70 milligrams; the average chocolate bar about 80. A 12-ounce bottle of cola contains up to 100 milligrams, about as much as a cup of coffee.

the true enemy

The current conclusions about the short-term psychological and physiological effects of caffeine are not so different from the first stabs in the dark by Arab physicians, or the conclusions arrived at by Dufour in the 17th century. But the long-term effects are not nearly so well understood, and are currently the subject of a vigorous, confusing, and so far inconclusive medical debate.

CAFFEINE

The short-term effects are, like the drug's history, paradoxical. The plus side is summed up by Dr. J. Murdoch Ritchie in the 1970 edition of *The Pharmacological Basis of Therapeutics:* Caffeine produces "a more rapid and clearer flow of thought," and allays "drowsiness and fatigue. After taking caffeine one is capable of a greater sustained intellectual effort and a more perfect association of ideas. There is also a keener appreciation of sensory stimuli, and . . . motor activity is increased; typists, for example, work faster and with fewer errors."

a keener appreciation

Such effects are produced by caffeine equivalent to the amount contained in one to two cups of coffee. According to Dr. Ritchie the same dosage stimulates the body in a variety of other ways: the heart rate increases, the blood vessels dilate; the movement of fluid and solid wastes through the body is promoted. All this adds up to the beloved "lift."

On the minus side, we have medical descriptions of the familiar "coffee nerves." The heavy coffee drinker may suffer from chronic anxiety, a sort of "coffee-come-down," and may be restless and irritable. As we all know, he may suffer from insomnia, and even twitching muscles and diarrhea. Really large doses of caffeine, the equivalent of about 10 cups of strong coffee drunk right in a row, produce genuinely toxic effects: vomiting, fever, chills, and mental confusion. And in enormous doses caffeine is quite literally deadly. The lethal dose of caffeine in humans is estimated at about 10 grams, or the equivalent of 100 cups of coffee. One would have to drink the 100 cups in one sitting, however, which doubtless accounts for the unpopularity of caffeine as a means of taking one's own life.

simple moderation

It would seem that the answer to the coffee paradox, at least so far as short-term effects are concerned, is simple moderation. Drunk to excess coffee is quite literally a poison; drunk in moderation it is still the beloved tonic of tradition, a gentle aid to thought, labor, and conversation.

But just how much is just enough and how much is too much? Exactly where is caffeine's golden mean? No study will commit itself. I can only offer a consensus estimate based on inference. I found, for instance, no study reporting negative effects from doses of caffeine under 300 milligrams a day. Since the average cup of coffee contains about 100 milligrams of caffeine, we could *infer* from this evidence that virtually anyone should be able to drink about three cups of coffee a day and enjoy the benefits of caffeine with none of the drawbacks. Such a figure assumes, of course, that one doesn't back the coffee up with a lot of cola drinks, chocolate bars, and headache pills. This is a conservative estimate, however. One could infer from other studies that five cups a day is safe for most people. Furthermore, response varies greatly from individual to individual; some people can't drink any amount of coffee comfortably.

none of the drawbacks

So much for short-term effects. Researchers in the last 10 years or so have also been busily trying to implicate coffee, particularly caffeine, in heart disease, birth defects, and a half dozen other less famous woes. So far, the evidence appears to be inconclusive. The clinical reports and studies I've skimmed through offer far more questions than answers, and for every report tentatively claiming a link between caffeine and some disease there seems to be another contradicting the first.

The one exception may be the possible link between birth defects and heavy caffeine intake in women during pregnancy. Experiments have indicated that the equivalent of 12 to 24 cups of coffee (or bottles of cola) per day may cause birth defects—in rats. Which is the catch, since human beings metabolize caffeine differently from rats, and studies of human beings so far do not collaborate the evidence found in the rat experiments. Further studies are being undertaken, but results will not be available until 1984 or 1985.

the catch

Even if the studies were to find a link between birth defects and such extremely heavy coffee drinking, no new advice would be indicated, since most physicians already tell pregnant women to avoid *any* drug, including caffeine, during pregnancy. Furthermore, nothing in these studies contradicts the three-cup-a-day moderation rule I introduced earlier.

CAFFEINE

Nevertheless, anyone who drinks a regular caffeinated coffee and also is pregnant, or takes tranquilizers, or suffers from ulcers or heart complaints, certainly ought to bring his or her coffee drinking habits to the attention of a physician for evaluation.

In light of the continuing conflicts in the medical evidence, why are so many people so *eager* to pin blame on coffee? Partly, I think, because of the frustrations of dealing with degenerative diseases with multiple causes, like heart failure. It would be marvellous to find a simple dietary "cause" like coffee, and one that doesn't even have any food value! There is a tendency, in other words, in the face of our impotence before certain diseases, to cast about for dietary scapegoats. Coffee is ideal for such a role, not only because it has no food value, but because it makes us feel good for no reason when we drink it. When we get sick I suspect we tend to fix the blame on something we already feel guilty about: coffee, wine, cake, or whatever.

a dietary scapegoat

The ease with which the early persecutions of coffee on religious grounds eased into condemnations on medical grounds makes the motivation behind the latest attacks on the healthfulness of coffee doubly suspect. Every culture or religion has its dietary taboos as well as its sacraments. Thou shalt not eat pork, or white bread, or meat on Fridays, or bananas on Wednesdays. A group which wishes to define its own identity must establish taboos. In the late sixties, an entire generation seemed busy trying to define itself as a culture distinct from the larger Western tradition. It was natural that coffee, as a social drug firmly identified with the establishment, should come under attack.

an establishment drug

I recall, for instance, visiting an early commune where ingesting caffeine was a spiritual and dietary sin almost as bad as closing the door to undress. Yet these same puritans, so critical of caffeine, regularly reduced themselves to monosyllabic incoherence with marijuana. I recall, too, an incident at my coffee house. A customer whose age and dress indicated he was definitely not a member of the establishment told me at length why he didn't want coffee: The caffeine was bad for people. He then ordered yerba maté tea, a pot of which contains at least as much caffeine as a mug of coffee. I told him so; he professed great interest, but still drank his maté tea. At the risk of projecting, I think his real reason for not drinking coffee was he assumed Richard Nixon, then President Nixon, drank coffee, whereas President Nixon had undoubtedly never *heard* of yerba maté tea.

These stories are not intended as criticism of the aspirations of the old counter-culture, but to point out that dietary choices, particularly of non-nutritive, mood-altering frills like coffee, are essentially irrational, arbitrary choices more akin psychologically to the fiats of religious belief or cultural prejudice than the reason of medical science. But since we live in an ostensibly rationally run, secular society, no one feels comfortable justifying his dietary prejudices on religious or cultural grounds. Instead he elevates some very tentative medical evidence into a dogma which he then defends as *a dogma* "scientific." Once upon a time foods were bad for the soul; now they're bad for our health. Medicine has become, in some circles, a front for religious or cultural snobbery.

Virtually every element in our diet is currently suspect on some medical grounds or other. At a time when the average glass of drinking water is suspected of harboring carcinogens, a once country-pure herbal tea like sassafras taken off the market because it contains a proven carcinogen, and large doses of vitamin C suspected in birth defects, I see little medical reason for not drinking moderate amounts of a beverage against which nothing concrete has been proven, which has been consumed for centuries without decimating the population, and which is one of the few widely consumed modern foods which contains no multisyllabic preservatives, additives, or other adulterants.

For the ordinary coffee drinker, I think the real solution to the health dilemma is to start treating coffee with the love and attention it deserves. If *love and attention* one pays attention to what one's doing when one buys and makes coffee, and takes a moment to appreciate the results, many of the supposed negative effects of coffee drinking might vanish. If anyone suffers from coffee, it's the unconscious coffeeholic who wanders around all day with a half-filled cup of cold dishwater in his hand. I doubt whether someone who genuinely and sensually loves coffee will abuse it, any more than someone who really loves his automobile will drive recklessly.

DECAFFEINATED
COFFEE

Technology to my mind is a marvelous bourgeois invention for having your cake and eating it, too. So you like coffee but not caffeine? Well then, we'll take out the caffeine and leave you your pleasure, intact. As always, technology is trying to take the bugs out of nature, and give us the garden back without the snake.

Decaffeinated coffee is indeed without venom; it contains at most one-fortieth the amount of caffeine in untreated beans, or only three percent of the original caffeine. Furthermore, the decaffeination process apparently reduces the amounts of other components of the bean which may or may not contribute to the deleterious effects coffee has on some persons.

Nor should the removal of caffeine alone alter the taste of coffee. Isolated, caffeine is a crystalline substance with no aroma and only the slightest bitter taste. As a flavoring agent it is manifestly lost in all the heady perfumes of fresh coffee. So if you hear someone say, "Coffee doesn't taste like coffee without the caffeine," he's wrong. The only real problem is how

flavor

to take out the caffeine without ruining the rest of what *does* influence coffee flavor. But technology has triumphed, more or less. The best decaffeinated coffee, fresh roasted and ground and carefully brewed, can taste so nearly the equal of a similar untreated coffee that only a tasting involving direct comparison will reveal the difference. Unfortunately, fine decaffeinated coffees are the exception rather than the norm. Decaffeinated beans are notoriously difficult to roast, and the roasting may be at fault when you buy a decaffeinated coffee that turns out to be thin bodied and tasteless.

Still, anything's better than Postum, and you can always spruce up a listless caffeine-free coffee by adding a little of one of the full-bodied coffees before grinding.

Most caffeine-free coffee sold in specialty stores is shipped from the growing countries to decaffeinating plants in Switzerland and Germany, *Switzerland* treated to remove the caffeine, then redried and shipped to the United *and Germany* States. The caffeine, by the way, is sold to manufacturers of medicines and soft drinks, who in turn sell their goods to people who may well have sworn off coffee.

Coffee is decaffeinated in its green state, before the delicate oils are developed through roasting. There are scores of patents for decaffeination processes, but those which are actually used apparently fall into one of three categories. In the older processes the beans are first steamed to open their pores, then soaked in an organic solvent which dissolves the caffeine. The beans are then again steamed to remove the solvent residues, dried, and roasted like any other green coffee.

This process has an obvious drawback: Minute quantities of the solvent may remain in the bean, spoiling flavor and ruining the day of any health *the solvent* fanatic who finds out about it. A process developed later simply soaks the green beans in hot (almost boiling) water for several hours. The water is then transferred to another tank where it is combined with a solvent which absorbs most of the caffeine. The caffeine-laden solvent is then separated from the *water*. The solvent is much easier to remove from water than from beans, because the solvent is lighter than water and never really mixes with it, whereas certain oils in the beans may actually selectively combine with the solvent, making it impossible to remove entirely.

The water is now free of both caffeine and solvent, but still contains oils and other materials important to flavor. In order not to lose these

CAFFEINE

materials, the water is returned to the first tank, where it is reabsorbed by the green beans.

The joker in the whole business is still the solvent. People who worry about the effects of coffee on their health are obviously not going to feel comfortable purchasing a product containing even minute traces of solvent (just what *does* it dissolve? brain cells; stomach tissue?). And then our worst fears were confirmed: One of the most widely used solvents, trichlorethylene, was named a probable cause of cancer in a "Cancer Alert" issued in 1975 by the National Cancer Institute. The "Alert" was aimed at the potential health hazards trichlorethylene poses to people who work around it rather than to consumers of decaffeinated coffees, since the solvent remains in coffee in extremely minute traces. The United States Federal Food and Drug Administration, for example, permits the solvent in quantities up to 10 parts per million in ground coffee. By comparison, the doses the Cancer Institute administered to their laboratory animals were gargantuan. To match them in equivalent terms, a human being would have to drink twenty million cups of decaffeinated coffee a day for his entire life. Also, we don't know how much of the solvent residue—if any—actually makes it through the brewing process to end up in the cup.

trichlorethylene

Nevertheless, the notion that the caffeine we feared caused heart disease was being replaced by a solvent that did cause cancer threw everyone who had been virtuously drinking caffeine-free coffee for years into consternation. The American coffee industry responded by replacing trichlorethylene with methylene chloride, a solvent not implicated in the National Cancer Institute's study. Just because methylene chloride did not figure in the study does not mean it is safe, however, only unpublicized. At this writing it too is being tested by the Cancer Institute.

another solvent

Now the third method of decaffeination enters the picture, riding a white horse. In 1979 Coffex S.A., a Swiss firm with plants in several European countries, announced it has developed a decaffeination process using *water only;* i.e. no solvents whatsoever. Coffex will not discuss technical details, although it has generously publicized the results of a tasting by coffee professionals who claim that water-only decaffeinated coffees taste fresher and better than those decaffeinated by the solvent process.

water only decaffeination

At the moment this water-only decaffeinated coffee is becoming available in the United States, although at prices considerably higher than the already high-priced conventionally treated beans. In my own tastings I find coffee decaffeinated by the new water-only process has *less* flavor than coffee treated by the solvent method, though possibly more body.

Caffeine is not the only villain in the coffee controversy. The other is certain chemicals often lumped together under the term "acid." Some people simply don't like the acid or sour note in coffee, and claim it disturbs their stomachs. Still others claim it causes jitters; there are doubtless some, particularly in California, who feel it will lead to the end of the world. I suggest that instead of taking my word for it, you experiment. Does that sourness in coffee make you feel uncomfortable in tongue or tummy? Then what you may want is not coffee with the "acid" taken out, but either a good dark-roasted coffee or a blended aged coffee. Dark roasting burns out most of the chemicals which cause the "acid" sensation, and aging mutes them. If you do your own blending, adding an old Java or aged coffee to your favorite straight coffee will produce a flavorful but very low-acid brew. There are also many coffees—some Venezuelan and Tanzania and most Mysore for example—which are naturally low on acid.

acid

By now you may be ready to switch to mint tea, if only you were sure it didn't cause mononucleosis in yaks. I can only urge you to treat coffee with love and respect, and hope that those among my readers who drink a lot of coffee without thinking will examine their habit, and those who worry too much about drinking moderate amounts of coffee will relax and enjoy their cup.

10 GROWING IT
How coffee is grown, processed, and graded

TO IMAGINE a coffee tree think of a camellia bush with flowers like a jasmine. The leaves look like the camellia's: broad, dark, shiny, and shaped like an arrow or spearhead. They are three to six inches long, and line up in pairs on either side of a central stem. The flowers—small, white star-shaped blossoms born in clusters at the base of the leaves—produce an exquisite, slightly bitter scent. The flower's white color and nocturnal aroma suggest the coffee plant prefers to be pollinated by moths or other night-flying insects, but in fact the plant largely pollinates itself. In freshly roasted coffee a hint of the flower fragrance seems to shimmer delicately within the darker perfumes of the brew. The arabica plant is an evergreen; in the wild it grows to a height of 14 to 20 feet, but when cultivated it is usually kept pruned to about six feet to facilitate picking the beans and to encourage heavy bearing.

the coffee tree

In some regions, Brazil for example, where there are one or two rainy seasons each year followed by dry seasons, the hills of the plantations whiten with blossoms all at once. In areas where there is an even rainfall all year round, blossoms, green berries, and ripe berries all cohabit the trees simultaneously. The scent of an entire coffee plantation in bloom can be so

161

GROWING IT

intense sailors have said the perfume reached them two or three miles out to sea. Such glory is short-lived, however; three or four days later the petals are strewn on the ground and the small coffee berries, or cherries as they are called in the trade, are forming in clusters at the base of the leaves.

small cherry

In six or seven months the berries have matured; they are oval, about the color and size of a small cherry. Within the skin and pulp are two coffee beans nestled with their flat sides together. Occasionally, as in liberated households, there are three seeds in one berry, but even more often just one, which grows small and round, and is sold in the trade as "peaberry" coffee. Each tree can produce between one and 12 pounds of coffee per year, depending on soil, climate, and other factors. The plants are propagated either from seed or cuttings. If propagated from seed a tree will take about three years to bear, and six to mature.

no extremes

Coffea arabica grows wild in the mountain rain forests of Ethiopia, where it inhabits the forest's middle tier, halfway between the ground cover and the taller trees. It will grow best wherever similar conditions prevail: no frost, but no hot extremes either; fertile, well-watered but well-drained soil (soil of volcanic origin seems best). Heavy rainfall will cause the trees to produce too much too fast and exhaust themselves; not enough rain and they will not flower or bear fruit. The trees require the same balance as regards direct sunlight: some but not too much; two hours a day seems ideal. The lacy leaves of the upper levels of the rain forest originally shaded the coffee tree; today some growers plant shade trees; others make trellis arrangements, or plant on hillsides which receive sun for only part of the day. In some mountainous areas, like the Kona coast of Hawaii, a light cloud cover forms regularly for part of the day, providing an "automatic shade."

hard bean

Whereas arabica trees planted at lower altitudes in the tropics will overbear, weaken, and fall prey to disease, trees grown at higher altitudes, around 3,000 to 6,000 feet, will usually produce coffee with a "hard bean." The slower-maturing berry produces a smaller, denser bean, less porous, containing less moisture and more flavor. We must beware, however, of easy distinctions. Some of the greatest coffees are soft bean, particularly Sumatran Mandheling and Celebes.

Coffee is sometimes grown on vast plantations, as in Brazil, where there are privately-owned *fazendas* with well over a million trees. Here processing is done on the plantation itself. Other, usually higher quality coffees, are grown on "estates," or small-to medium-sized farms. Excellent coffees are also grown by small peasant farmers in patches of a few acres at most, and processed through cooperatives. The farmer grows food crops for subsistence, and some coffee for exchange. The cooperatives, often government-sponsored, attempt to maintain and improve growing practices and grading standards.

Harvesting is one of the most important factors in how coffee tastes. Coffee berries, with the usual individualism of the brew, do not ripen uniformly. The same branch may at the same moment display ripe red berries, unripe green berries, and overripe black berries. So the conscientious grower who wants to get a high price for his coffee will pick the berries selectively; he will go over his trees again and again picking only ripe berries. Where coffee is carelessly harvested, the berries are stripped just once from the tree, ripe, unripe, and overripe all together.

harvesting

Once it is picked, coffee can be prepared either by the "dry" method, which produces what is called "natural" coffee, or by the "wet" method, which produces "washed" coffee. The "dry" method, which is the older, more primitive method, simply involves drying the berries in the sun or in a mechanical dryer, and later stripping the hard, shriveled husk off the bean, either by modern machine or with a grindstone or mortar and pestle.

dry preparation

The wet method removes most of the covering from the bean *before* it is dried. Since the moist bean is liable to damage if treated roughly, the covering must be removed gingerly, layer by layer. First the skin and pulp are gently stripped off by machine. This leaves the beans covered with a sticky, gluey substance, which if removed mechanically, would damage the

wet preparation

bean. Instead, the beans are soaked, and natural enzymes literally digest or ferment this slimy layer off the bean. This step is called "fermentation."

Next, the coffee is gently washed, and finally dried, either by the sun in open terraces, where it is continuously turned and stirred by workers, or in large mechanical driers. This leaves a last thin skin covering the bean, *"pergamino"* called the "parchment" or "pergamino." If all has gone well, the parchment will be thoroughly dry and crumbly, and as easily removed as the skin from a peanut. Some coffee is sold and shipped in its parchment cover, "en pergamino," but most often a last machine called a "huller" is used to remove it before shipping. The huller is also designed to polish the coffee, giving the flinty, dry beans a clean, glossy look especially important to specialty roasters, who sell their coffee in whole bean.

The wet method is not widely used in countries like Brazil where the coffee berries ripen nearly all at once, since the labor and machinery necessary to wet process a single gigantic crop of coffee is prohibitive. In other parts of the world, Colombia for instance, there is plentiful rainfall all year round, and coffee ripens and can be processed continuously; consequently fewer workers can process more coffee, and do it better.

"Washed" coffee is not necessarily better than dry-processed or "natural" coffee. In some cases natural coffee may actually have a more distinctive flavor and more body, apparently owing to certain enzymes which remain in close contact with the bean throughout the drying process. Nevertheless, *more can go wrong* much more can go wrong with natural coffee than with washed coffee. Since drying the entire berry takes so much longer than drying washed beans, any green berries mixed with the ripe will have more opportunity to rot and impart a foul taste to the rest of the ripe berries. More importantly, most natural coffee is also strip-picked, which means there will *always* be some contamination of flavor by green or overripe berries. Most natural coffee is also dried carelessly. Processed with *care*, however, natural coffees can be as good or better than washed coffee. Most coffees carried by your specialty coffee store are washed coffees. The main exception is Arabian Mocha, and

DRYING COFFEE BERRIES

possibly some Ethiopian coffees, which despite primitive methods, are picked and handled with care, and are the equal of the best washed coffees.

The last step in processing is cleaning. With high-quality coffees, the beans are run on conveyor belts past workers, usually women (the wives of the men who are out moving the coffee around), who hand-pick defective beans, sticks, dirt, and other debris from the sound beans. Commercial coffees are machine-cleaned; by the time a stick or bad bean reaches you it will be ground up or freeze-dried anyhow, so only the taste buds will know. Coffee which has been picked over by hand is usually called "European preparation"; all specialty coffees, since they are whole bean and the consumer sees what he gets, will be European preparation.

European preparation

Before marketing, coffee must be graded. Approaches differ from country to country, but there are four main criteria: how big the bean is, where (and at what altitude) it was grown, how it was prepared and picked, and how good it tastes, or cup quality. In some instances coffees are also graded by the number of "imperfections" (meaning defective and broken beans, pebbles, sticks, etc.) per kilogram. I've included more information on grading by country in Chapter 3.

GROWING YOUR OWN

The more enthusiastic among my readers may decide to begin growing their own if coffee prices keep rising; unfortunately, this is a dream few of us are in a position to realize. A true devotee of the bean would need a commercial-size greenhouse or a good-sized back yard in or near the tropics to remain well-disposed every morning the year round. First one needs a frost-free environment; this eliminates most back yards in the United States. Then figure one mature tree trimmed to about six feet should produce an average of two to four pounds of coffee a year. Including the decaffeinated coffee I consume, it would take six to eight such trees to keep me jolly. Better grow vegetables.

However, if you want just a small specimen with a few leaves to stroke in the morning and make thankful offerings to, you will have no problem.

The *Coffea arabica* is easy to grow indoors, and makes a very attractive house plant. If it likes you enough it will even reward you with flowers and berries. You can start your coffee plant three ways. The easiest is to buy a seedling. Though it's not an extremely popular house plant, most indoor nurseries carry the arabica at least occasionally. The next easiest method is to take a clipping from a friend's plant and root it. Finally, you can plant some green coffee beans, and wait ... and wait.... Fresh beans sprout in about three or four weeks, but obviously the green beans that reach you through your corner coffee store will be at least a couple of months old. But if you're patient, and you plant a *lot* of beans (most won't germinate at all, ever), you might eventually have yourself a plantation.

a house plant

Beans should be planted a little over a half-inch deep, in good, well-drained potting soil, and kept moist at all times, but not wet. When you have something that looks like a plant, treat it as you would a camellia: rich, well-drained soil, always moist but never wet, with plenty of bright indirect, or diffused sunlight. Fertilize every other month. If something goes wrong, look up camellia in a good gardening manual for the appropriate advice.

If you do live in a *totally* frost-free area you might well want to plant some arabica in your yard. Temperatures should not be lower than 60° normally, and lower than 50° for short periods only. Parts of Hawaii are unsurpassed for coffee, and it has long been held that coffee could be successfully grown commercially along the California coast, but never tried because of high labor costs. Remember, however, that you need to duplicate the conditions of the Ethiopian rain forest: moist, fertile, well-drained soil and partial shade; this last would be especially important during the long summers in southern California. For more advice on growing, pruning (very important if you wish your tree to produce more coffee), and caring for coffee trees, read A. E. Haarer's *Coffee Growing* in the Oxford Tropical Handbooks series, Oxford University Press.

in your yard

11 COFFEE HOUSES
How to get it when you're out, have fun, and threaten the establishment

EVERY SOCIAL LUBRICANT has its home away from home, its church, as it were, where its effects are celebrated in public ceremonies and ritual conviviality. Alcohol has its bars, saloons, and dance halls, and opium its dens. The café or coffee house, the social home of coffee, is literally as old as the beverage itself. The first people to enjoy coffee as a beverage rather than medicine or aid to meditation apparently did so in coffee houses in Mecca in the late 15th century. The nature of the coffee house was established early, and has changed remarkably little in 500 years.

Jean de Thévenot describes a Turkish coffee house of 1664 in his *Relation d'un voyage fait au Levant:* "There are public coffee houses where the drink is prepared in very big pots for the numerous guests. At these places guests mingle without distinction of rank or creed; nor does anyone think it amiss to enter such places, where people go to pass their leisure time. In front of the coffee-houses are benches with small mats, where those sit who would rather remain in the fresh air and amuse themselves by watching the passers-by. Sometimes the coffee-house keeper engages flute-players and violin-players, and also singers, to entertain his guests."

a Turkish coffee house

COFFEE HOUSES

The "very big pots" of De Thévenot's café have become today's espresso machines or coffee urns, the "benches with small mats," outdoor terraces. And though the café shares many qualities with the bars, saloons, and *boîtes* beloved of drinkers of spirits, it has maintained its own subtly unique identity.

social gestalt

The peculiar social gestalt of the café appears to be intimately connected to the effect coffee and caffeine have on the nervous system. Coffee provokes conscious or mental associations, whereas alcohol, for instance, provokes automatic or instinctual associations. In other words, alcohol typically makes us want to eat, fight, make love, dance, and sleep, whereas coffee encourages us to think, talk, read, write, or work. We drink wine to relax, and coffee to drive home. For the Moslems, the world's first coffee

"wine of Apollo"

drinkers, coffee was the "wine of Apollo," the beverage of thought, dream, and dialectic, "the milk of thinkers and chess players." It was the faithful Moslem's answer to the other wine, the Christian and pagan wine of Dionysus and ecstasy.

Hence the customers of coffee houses from their inception in Mecca down to the present tend to talk and read rather than dance, play chess rather than gamble, and listen contemplatively to music rather than sing themselves. The café also has a greater tendency to open itself to the street and sun than bars or saloons, whose walls and darknesses protect the drinker against the encroachment of the sober, workaday world. Rather than subterranean refuge, the coffee drinker wants a comfortable corner from which to read his newspaper, observe, and pass judgement on the world as it slips by, just beyond the edge of his table.

informal study

The café is intimately connected with work (the truck stop, the coffee break), and with its own special brand of informal study and intellectual loafing. A customer with his nose buried in reading matter is a common sight in even the most low-brow cafe. The Turks called their cafés "schools of the wise." In 17th- century England coffee houses were often called "penny universities"; for the price of entry (one penny; coffee cost two, which included newspapers) one could participate in a floating seminar which might very well include the likes of Addison and Steele. As a matter of fact, aside from the Romanticists, who temporarily switched to mountaintops, it's hard to find a famous European intellectual who didn't seem to spend the better part of his days in cafés or coffee houses. The Renaissance not only gave Europe a new world view, but coffee, tea, and cocoa as well. It must have been rather difficult to consider revolutionizing Western thought after the typical medieval breakfast of beer and herring.

The ideas which have issued from the cafés of history have usually been in the direction of change rather than maintenance of the status quo. Both the French and American revolutions are said to have been nurtured in cafés The speech which led to the storming of the Bastille took place in the Café Foy, and Daniel Webster called the Green Dragon, a famous Boston coffee house, "the headquarters of the revolution." Since coffee does encourage thought, we may very well consider it a radical beverage, as thinking leads so inevitably to invidious comparisons between what is and what could be.

revolutions

At any rate, persecutions of coffee drinking and cafés have always been tinged by politics. Once tyrants have controlled newspapers, their next goal is to suppress talk. Early persecutions sounded religious, but very rapidly became overtly political. The governor of Mecca repressed the very first coffee houses in 1511 because "in these places men and women meet and play violins, tambourines, . . . chess . . . and do other things contrary to our sacred law." This repression, like the rest, was short-lived. Repressions followed in Cairo, and the Grand Vizier of Constantinople ordered the coffee houses of that city closed around 1600 because he said they encouraged sedition. He let the saloons stay open, however. Caught drinking your first illegal cup of coffee, you got beaten with a stick; for the second, you got sewn in a leather bag and dumped in the Bosphorus. But even such definite measures didn't stop the coffee drinkers. Floating coffee houses developed; enterprising people walked around with pots of the brew and set up for quickies in alleys and behind buildings.

persecutions

COFFEE HOUSES

In 1675 King Charles II of England published an edict closing coffee houses, the apparent pretext being an extraordinary document entitled *The Women's Petition Against Coffee, representing to public consideration the grand inconveniences accruing to their sex from the excessive use of the drying and enfeebling Liquor.* Conscientiously supporting their thesis with abundant example and plentiful detail, the authors contended that since becoming coffee drinkers, their men had become "as unfruitful as the deserts, from whence that unhappy berry is said to be brought," and that as a consequence, "the whole race is in danger of extinction." This insinuation, as readers of Chapter 9 are already aware, was a typically below-the-belt stratagem among early-day coffee-haters. The men rose to the occasion, however, with *The Men's Answer to the Women's Petition . . . vindicating their liquor from the undeserved aspersion lately cast upon them, in their scandalous pamphlet.*

as unfruitful as the deserts

But, however interested he may have been in questions of virility, Charles' real concerns were revealed in the wording of his *Proclamation:* " . . . in such Houses . . . divers False, Malitious and Scandalous Reports are devised and spread abroad, to the Defamation of his Majestie's Government, and to the Disturbance of the Peace and Quiet of the Realm." The reaction among coffee-lovers was pronounced and immediate, and only 11 days later Charles published a second edict withdrawing his first, *An Additional Proclamation Concerning Coffee Houses,* declaring that he had decided to allow them to stay open out of "Royal Compassion." Some observers cite this turnaround as a record for the most words eaten in the shortest time by any ruler of a major nation, unsurpassed until modern times.

Royal Compassion

The *caffè* in Italian, *café* in French, *kahveh kane* in Turkish, are variously coffee shops, coffee houses, cafes, cafés, and sometimes caffès in North America. The variety of names is not quite meaningless. Coffee *shops* are usually plastic and formica places where people go to eat light meals and drink a decent, but hardly distinguished, cup of coffee, usually a cheap blended coffee roasted to North American tastes, brewed weak. Cafe is a more ambiguous term; on one extreme it describes a heartier, more down-home version of the coffee shop, with more enameled wood and less formica, which in its individualism may serve coffee anywhere from excellent to the most abysmal brew this side of the army.

But when we get to the other extreme of "café," the kind with the accent *aigu* over the "e," we leave the world of the mainstream North American coffee drinker behind and enter the world of the cappuccino and croissant. In this world "café" usually describes a fairly pretentious French-style place with espresso, marble-top tables, large windows, and a clean, well-lighted look. The "caffè" is an Italian-speaking "café"; it's also usually bright and clean, and always has an espresso machine.

the café

But the "coffee house" is another matter; like cafés and caffès it usually sports an espresso machine, but stays open later, tends to be a little darker and a little dirtier than its counterparts, and offers beer, wine, and entertainment. Cafés and caffès tend to be opened in resorts and busy cities by first- and second-generation European-Americans; coffee houses tend to be opened by young idealists with non-conforming life styles anywhere they can find cheap rent and some other young idealists. Coffee houses are often supported by radical political groups and liberal churches, in an effort to "reach the youth," or they may be run and owned collectively.

the coffee house

Lately, with the idealistic generation of the 60's turning into monied young professionals and high-style homemakers, coffee houses are going out of vogue, while cafés, caffès, and various other interpretations of European style hangouts are popping up wherever picturesque old neighborhoods are turning into chic new neighborhoods. Although the principal reading material in such places appears to be the menu, and the leading intellectual exercise choosing a dessert, I feel that where there are coffee and marbletop tables there's hope. If the *cappuccini* keep improving, great ideas, revolution, and good poetry may appear again on boutique row.

12 COFFEE DRINKS
Fancy, fortified, cold, and flaming coffees

This is a chapter of recipes, limited, however, to liquid recipes. They are divided into three groups: unusual hot coffee drinks, coffee drinks fortified with spirits, and iced coffee drinks.

SOME NOTES ON INGREDIENTS
Cocoa Use an unsweetened powder, as dark and perfumy as you can get. Many of the "instant hot chocolate" mixes on the market contain sugar, and even powdered milk. Besides being overpriced they are not concentrated enough to give the powerful penetration of chocolate a good mocha or other coffee-chocolate drink demands. A really good coffee specialty store should carry such a cocoa in bulk. If not, buy Hershey's. It is not as intense and flavorful as some bulk cocoas, but it is pure and widely available.

For drinks topped with foamed milk or whipped cream, keep unsweetened cocoa powder in a shaker next to your milk steamer or coffee pot. Garnish the white stuff with a few shakes. On foamed milk it melts and forms a delicate crust.

For mochas and other drinks calling for cocoa, add 1 heaping teaspoon of cocoa powder, 1 to 2 of brown sugar, and a little grated vanilla bean to a cup of milk; heat gently or steam while stirring. This makes an excellent hot chocolate drink, and 1/3 cup of it mixed with espresso and topped with foamed milk will make a mocha fit to make Voltaire drool in his grave.

Orange and lemon peel Most commercially grown oranges and lemons have been sprayed with insecticide; even if it's a "safe" insecticide, the skin may smell like it's been pickled in fly spray. Since the skin, not the juice or pulp, is used in coffee drinks for the sake of its intensely flavored oils, you would be wise to purchase untreated or "organic" oranges and lemons at your local natural foods store. They usually taste better, too.

Heating or steaming milk I describe the Italian or espresso method of heating milk, and the machines you do it with, in Chapter 7. Rather than heating milk from the bottom, over a flame, a sort of tube with a nozzle on the end is stuck into the milk and live steam issues out of the nozzle, gently heating the milk without imparting a boiled or heated taste, and, if you do it right, raising a head of froth or foam on top of the milk. No coffee drink made with hot milk will taste quite right unless you steam the milk, rather than heat it on the stove.

COFFEE DRINKS

Extra- and double-strength coffee
Some recipes call for a coffee made stronger than usual. For recipes calling for "extra-strength" coffee make it one-and-a-half times as strong as you would normally: 3 level tablespoons per 6-ounce cup if you follow standard practice. For double-strength make it twice as strong: 4 level tablespoons per 6-ounce cup.

UNUSUAL HOT COFFEE DRINKS

All over the world people combine large amounts of hot milk with their coffee. Fill a tall glass or small bowl with one part extra- to double-strength coffee and one part hot milk, steamed if possible. Top with a dash of cocoa powder, ground nutmeg, or grated orange peel and granulated sugar. If you make the coffee with regular or Viennese roast, it is *Kaffee Milch* (German). Made with espresso or Italian roast, it is *Caffè Latte* (Italian); with dark French roast coffee *Café au Lait* (French) or *Café con Leche* (Spanish).

Latin Americans like to make their coffee very, very strong, and heat it together with a very, very large proportion of milk. *New Orleans Coffee* is a participant in this tradition. Use a dark roast or chicory blend coffee. Brew it twice as strong as usual. Combine one part coffee with two parts hot milk (steamed if possible) in a tall glass or small bowl. What some people call *Mexican Coffee* is simply about one part very strong, dark-roast coffee combined with three parts hot milk.

Which brings us to coffees topped with whipped cream. Virtually any coffee tastes good this way. Make it a little stronger than usual, and serve it in a five- or six-ounce stemmed glass, the rather thick, substantial kind that tapers outward at the top and is used for Irish coffee and other fortified beverages. The glass will permit you to enjoy the contrast between the white cream and dark coffee. Use real whipped cream. The stuff in cans is too light; it will melt in hot coffee as fast as an early snow on a manhole cover. If you care to, you can top your coffee with partly whipped cream, Irish-coffee style: Whip the cream so it's thick but not stiff. If you sweeten your coffee, do it before you add the cream. Then slide the half-whipped cream onto the coffee so it floats on the surface; sip the coffee through the cold, thick cream.

To garnish drinks made with the lighter roasts of coffee, top the whipped cream with ground cinnamon, nutmeg, or cloves. For drinks made with the darker roasts, use cocoa powder or grated orange peel and granulated sugar. Made with a light- or moderate-roast coffee, this drink is often called *Viennese Coffee;* whipped cream also speaks other languages, as in *Espresso con Panna* (Italian: espresso coffee with whipped cream), or *Kaffee mit Schlag* (German: coffee with whipped cream).

Whipped egg whites also make an excellent topping for hot coffee. The distributors of the Cappuccin-Olà milk steamer give this recipe for *Café Belgique.* Beat 1 egg white and 1/4 teaspoon vanilla extract until stiff. Put 2 generously heaping teaspoons of this mixture in each cup, and add 1/2 cup moderate- or dark-roast coffee, brewed extra-strength, and 2 tablespoons half-and-half, heated (steamed if possible). The egg white will float to the top of the cup, stained with swirls of brown. If you have an espresso brewer, try it with espresso; decrease the amount of coffee and add some milk to the half-and-half.

My favorite combination for spiced coffee is clove and orange peel, with a little lemon peel to develop the flavor of the orange. I don't like cinnamon; it seems to go dead when combined with coffee and citrus (whereas it goes into exaltation combined with apple and wine). Nutmeg, allspice, and cardamom are also interesting with coffee, but go easy with the latter. For every cup of *Simple Spiced Coffee*, place 1 large strip orange peel, 1 small strip lemon peel and 10 whole cloves in the bottom part of a drip or filter coffee pot. Drip the coffee as usual. Sweeten to taste with brown sugar. Use regular or Viennese, rather than dark, roast coffee. A heavy-bodied coffee like Sumatran or Celebes would be best.

Coffee Grog is a pleasant winter notion; you can make the grog mix in advance, store it indefinitely in the refrigerator, and add it to freshly brewed coffee by the cup.

Grog mix:
2 tablespoons butter
1 cup brown sugar
dash salt
1/4 teaspoon each ground cloves
   and nutmeg

Cream the butter, add the other ingredients, and combine thoroughly. Store in an airtight jar in the refrigerator. When you're ready to drink some, make a heavy-bodied coffee, like a Sumatran or Celebes, extra-strength. Use a regular, not a dark roast.

To each cup:

1 to 2 teaspoons grog mix
1 large strip orange peel
1 small strip lemon peel
2 tablespoons heavy cream, heated or steamed
1/2 cup hot brewed coffee, made extra-strength

Combine the ingredients in a preheated mug, adding the coffee last.

FORTIFIED COFFEE DRINKS

Coffee and booze not only taste good together, they relax and invigorate in a single tasty operation. Spirits and coffee contradict yet complement one another, like hot fudge and vanilla ice cream. When you put them together you're putting together Christianity and Islam, Dionysus and Apollo, the cerebral and the instinctual. If you want something philosophical to muse over when you suck your Irish coffee through the whipped cream, try that.

The most traditional fortified drink is brandy and coffee. But almost any booze goes well with coffee, including most liqueurs and several wines. Some possibilities are: brandy, grappa, Calvados (apple brandy), Irish whiskey, Scotch whisky, light and dark rum, kümmel, anisette, Cointreau, Strega, Grand Marnier, kirsch, Tuaca, Curacao, crème de cacao, sherry, tawny port, and sweet vermouth.

Café Royale or Café Gloria is dark (French or Italian) roast coffee, served with a little sugar (about a teaspoon per glass) and a lot of brandy. Fortify it with Calvados, or apple brandy, and it becomes *Normandy Coffee.*

Irish Coffee belongs to a whole family of coffee drinks, all of which add a head of lightly whipped cream to sweetened, fortified coffee in a stemmed glass. Put a teaspoon, more or less, of sugar in the glass, fill halfway to the top with hot coffee (not a dark roast; use American or Viennese), and add an ounce or so of Irish whiskey (Scotch works too); then top with whipping cream which has been beaten until it's partly stiff, but still pours. It should be soft enough to float with an even line on the surface of the coffee, rather than bob around in lumps. If the cream tends to sink or mix with the coffee, pour it into a teaspoon held just at the surface of the coffee. Irish coffee should not be stirred; sip the hot coffee and whiskey through the cool whipped cream.

You can follow the same procedure with any of your favorite coffees and liquors; if you add brandy instead of Irish whiskey and use a darker-roast coffee it becomes *Venetian Coffee.* If you make it with crème de cacao it is *Café Cacao.* Beyond that point make up your own names.

The more complicated, large-scale drinks require advance planning (they laughed when I sat down at the chafing dish), and in some cases, rehearsal. There are two main kinds: those that use light rum as the main fortifying ingredient, and those that use brandy. The brandy drinks are usually made flaming, which is why I suggest a rehearsal, in the driveway if possible. Brandy burns with an evanescent, pure blue flame when lit. The sight of the flame at the table seldom fails to provoke after-dinner awe. Such drinks have to be concocted in the evening with the lights dim, however; in sunlight the flame becomes virtually invisible and the drama negligible.

Café Brûlot, Café Diable, and *Café Flambé* are all very similar drinks; in all cases a spiced brandy mixture is heated, lit, and combined with a strong after-dinner coffee. A richly flavored coffee is best, like a Colombian, Sumatran, or Yemen Mocha. Use a regular, rather than dark, roast. Before serving, this mixture needs to be gently heated and stirred to dissolve the sugar, and raise the temperature of the brandy. Brandy at cool room temperature won't ignite.

To each cup:

2 teaspoons sugar (try brown)
1-1/2 jiggers brandy
10 whole cloves
1 large strip orange peel
1 small strip lemon peel
1 cup hot brewed coffee, made extra-strength

Combine the sugar, brandy, cloves, and orange and lemon peels in a chafing dish. Stir gently to dissolve the sugar. Fill the glasses or cups two-thirds full of coffee, and place around the chafing dish. When the brandy has been gently warmed (you should be able to smell it very clearly from three feet away if it's ready), pass a lighted match over the chafing dish. The brandy should ignite. Let the brandy burn for as long as you get a reaction from your audience (but not over half a minute), then ladle over the coffee. The flame will usually die when the brandy is ladled into the glasses. *Don't let the brandy burn too long,* or the flame will consume all the alcohol.

If you don't have a chafing dish, put the sugar in each glass *before* you add the coffee; heat the brandy, cloves and citrus on the stove. When the fumes are rising, pour into a fancy bowl and bring to the table. Carefully lay an ounce or two of the brandy mixture atop each glass of coffee; if you pour the brandy gently it will float on the surface of the coffee. To ignite the brandy pass a match over each glass; to douse the flame mix the brandy and coffee.

If you have trouble getting the brandy to float, try holding a teaspoon right on the surface of the coffee, and pouring the brandy mixture onto the spoon, letting it spread from there over the surface of the coffee. Remember, too, to add the sugar to the *coffee*, not the brandy mixture, or the sugar will make the brandy too heavy to float. If you're serving only one or two cups, you can heat the brandy

mixture right in the ladle. Done right, this can make a smooth conclusion to an intimate dinner.

The same drink can be made with light rum. Follow the instructions I gave earlier, substituting rum for brandy, and omitting the flame business. Still another possibility is half rum and half brandy.

The best rum recipes, however, add butter and brown sugar, and are usually called coffee grog, or some other hearty nautical name. Here's a good one: Return to the recipe for coffee grog described earlier; spike it with a jigger of rum, brandy, or a mixture of both. Make sure that your coffee is hot and your mugs preheated, since the cream, spirits, and grog mix will rapidly cool lukewarm coffee.

And here is a faster, somewhat heartier *Coffee Grog.*

To each cup:

1/2 jigger each rum and brandy (or a whole jigger of either)
1 large strip orange peel
1 small strip lemon peel
10 whole cloves
dash of ground cinnamon or a bit of stick cinnamon
1/2 cup hot brewed coffee
1 to 2 teaspoons brown sugar

Rub the inside of mugs with butter. Combine the ingredients in a saucepan or chafing dish. Heat gently just short of boiling; pour into the buttered mugs, and add a jigger or so of heavy cream, or if you prefer, drink it black.

Remember too that you can add spirits to any of the drinks that come

without it; a shot of brandy is excellent in an espresso-type cappuccino, for instance; or try adding brandy, rum, or sherry to a mocha.

COFFEE LIQUEUR

Styles of coffee liqueurs differ. Before making your own I suggest you try the two best (for my money) commercial coffee liqueurs available, Kahlúa and Chase and Sanborn. Kahlúa is heavy-bodied and based on a dark roast coffee blend; the Chase and Sanborn liqueur is somewhat lighter in body and based on a medium roast coffee. If you lean towards Kahlúa, use a dark roast coffee and go a little heavier on the vanilla and (if you use it) glycerin in the recipe below; if you prefer Chase and Sanborn, use a medium roast, acidy coffee, like a Colombian and go a little lighter on the vanilla and glycerin. You might also experiment with the sugar; the touch of molasses in brown sugar will make a heavier flavored liqueur. Your liqueur will never taste quite like the best commercial products, but you may end up liking it as well or better. Store your liqueur in tightly capped bottles in the refrigerator.

1 part finely ground, dark-roast coffee
1 part brown sugar
1 part 90 to 100 proof vodka
1 inch fresh vanilla bean per cup of ground coffee

Use a filter cone or pot to make the coffee. Heat the *same* quantity of hot water as you have coffee; in other words, if you have 2 cups of ground coffee in your coffee cone prepare only 2 cups of hot water. Slit the vanilla bean and allow it to simmer in the brewing water for 15 minutes or so. Fish it out again before you pour the water over the coffee and save it.

Pour the water over the coffee slowly, to make sure you wet all the grounds. Then pour the resulting concentrated coffee through the grounds a second time. Immediately dissolve the sugar in the hot concentrate. Add the vodka and the vanilla bean, and refrigerate in a stoppered bottle for a few days. Taste; when you can barely distinguish the vanilla tint, pour into a second bottle (or some glasses) and dispose of the vanilla bean. If you're impatient, substitute vanilla extract for the bean. Add 2 or 3 drops per cup of vodka any time after you've brewed the coffee. Variations: Substitute light rum for the vodka, or add a dash of tequila to every cup of rum or vodka. If you want your liqueur to have the very heavy body of the commercial stuff, add 2 teaspoons of glycerine.

The simple addition of chocolate turns coffee liqueur into *Mocha Liqueur*. Thoroughly mix one part hot water and one part unsweetened cocoa powder. Add 1/2 tablespoon of this mixture to every cup of the finished coffee liqueur.

ICED COFFEE DRINKS

The trick to iced coffee drinks is to make the coffee extra-strength, at least one-and-one-half again as strong as usual, so when the ice melts your coffee won't taste watery. *Café Mazagran*

is strong French-roast coffee poured over ice, served with club soda on the side. Sweeten and add the soda to taste. This drink was named after a fortress in Algeria where the Foreign Legionnaires supposedly invented it while torturing Bedouins and having mysteriously elliptical conversations with Sidney Greenstreet. This classic drink may well make you feel like Humphrey Bogart, particularly if you serve the soda in a syphon and the coffee in tall glasses.

Spiced Iced Coffee is an excellent idea. For each cup, put 1 large strip orange peel, 1 small strip lemon peel, and 5 whole cloves in the bottom of your drip or filter brewer. Make the coffee about half-again as strong as usual, and chill spice and citrus and all, in a closed jar. The refrigeration will make the coffee even spicier; pour over ice in tall glasses. Serve with half-and-half and brown sugar, or sweeten it first and top with whipped cream.

If you have a blender you can blend ice, coffee, and whatever else you want into a single cold creamy coffee sensation. There is no tradition behind blended coffee drinks, so everyone makes up names of his own. I'll call this one *Creamy Iced Coffee*:

1 cup chilled brewed coffee, made double-strength
2 rounded tablespoons confectioners' sugar
3 cups chopped ice

Combine the coffee, sugar, and ice, and blend until creamy. To make what I would like to call *Creamy Café au Lait*, add 1 cup half-and-half. To take your blender to the continent, use a

dark-roast coffee. Another variation: Add 2 rounded teaspoons malt powder, plain or chocolate.

You can of course add ice cream as well as whipped cream to strong iced coffee. I'm sure your imagination is quite up to it (cherries? nuts?), but in case you're blocked, here is a simple suggestion from the Caffè Mediterraneum in Berkeley; they call it a *Berliner*. Fill a tall glass halfway up with chilled Viennese (or any roast) coffee. Add a big scoop of chocolate ice cream, and top with whipped cream and a dash of cocoa powder.

Finally, you can either add spirits to many of these cold drinks, or chill the hot drinks before you add the spirits. The café cacao I mentioned earlier makes an excellent cold drink. Brew the coffee in advance and chill; mix a jigger of crème de cacao and a few ounces of coffee in a stemmed glass and top with whipped cream. Dust with cocoa powder or grated orange peel and sugar: *Chilled Café Cacao*.

Or return to the recipe for creamy café au lait. Add 2 jiggers Cointreau or Grand Marnier and 1/4 teaspoon grated orange peel, then blend: *Creamy Café Cointreau*. Cold, fortified coffee drinks are easy to invent, and a good outlet for frustrated creativity, not to mention fulfilled drunkenness. Carry on.

Don't forget that all of these dessert drinks and fortified coffees can be made with decaffeinated coffee, should you wish to revel in flavor alone and go to bed early.

WORDS FOR IT
A glossary

AA Capped letters are grade indicators usually describing the size of the bean. In Peru, for example, AAA is the largest bean; in Kenya, Tanzania and New Guinea AA; in India A.

ABYSSINIAN Former name for Ethiopia, and occasionally still applied to the lesser wild or gathered coffees from that country.

ACIDY The pleasant tartness of a fine coffee. Acid is also used to describe coffee components which ostensibly produce indigestion or nervousness in some individuals, or more precisely, to describe the actual, chemically defined acids present in coffee.

AFTER-DINNER ROAST A roast of coffee, dark brown with a bittersweet tang.

AGED COFFEE Coffee held in special warehouses for long periods. Aging reduces acidity and increases body.

ALAJUELA One of the better coffees of Costa Rica.

ALTURA "Heights" in Spanish; describes Mexican coffee which has been high or mountain grown.

AMERICAN ROAST Coffee roasted to North American tastes: medium brown.

ANKOLA One of the best coffees of Sumatra.

ANTIGUA One of the best coffees of Guatemala.

ARABIAN MOCHA Straight coffee from the southwestern tip of the Arabian peninsula, present-day Yeman.

ARABICA, COFFEA ARABICA The earliest cultivated species of coffee tree, and still most widely grown.

ARMENIA One of the better coffees of Colombia.

AROMA Describes the odor of freshly brewed coffee.

ARUSHA Coffee from the slopes of Mt. Meru in Tanzania.

AUTOMATIC FILTER COFFEE MAKERS Coffee brewers which automatically heat and measure water into a filter receptacle containing the ground coffee.

BARAHONA One of the best coffees of the Dominican Republic.

BATCH ROASTER Apparatus which roasts a given quantity ("batch") of coffee at a time.

BLEND A mixture of two or more straight coffees.

BODY The sense of heaviness, richness or thickness when one tastes coffee.

BOGOTÁ One of the best coffees of Colombia.

BOURBON A botanical vaiety of Coffea arabica which first appeared on the island of Bourbon, now Réunion. Some of the best Mexican and Brazilian coffees, among others, are from Bourbon stock.

BOURBON SANTOS The finest Brazilian coffee.

BRAZILIAN Straight coffee from Brazil, but more specifically, a cheap, naturally processed, fair to poor arabica coffee used until recently as the basis for most American commercial blends. Coffee sold as Brazilian in most specialty stores is a higher-grade coffee, Bourbon Santos.

BROWN ROAST Coffee roasted to North American tastes: medium brown.

BUCARAMANGA An excellent but uncharacteristically low-acid coffee from Colombia.

BUGISHU Arabica coffee from the slopes of Mt. Elgon in Uganda.

CAFFEINE The chemical agent responsible for the stimulating effect of coffee and tea; an odorless, bitter alkaloid.

CARACOL See Peaberry.

CARACAS A class of coffees from Venezuela, ranging from fair to excellent in quality.

CELEBES Straight coffee from the island of Celebes, Indonesia, now Sulawesi.

CHANCHAMAYO One of the best straight coffees of Peru.

CHICORY The root of the endive, roasted and ground like coffee.

CHINA YUNNAN Straight coffee from China.

CINNAMON ROAST Coffee roasted slightly lighter than the North American norm.

CITY ROAST, FULL CITY ROAST Coffee roasted slightly darker than the North American norm.

COATEPEC, ALTURA COATEPEC. Coffee from the central mountain range in south central Mexico, Veracruz State.

COBAN One of the best coffees of Guatemala.

COFFEOL, COFFEE OIL, COFFEE ESSENCE The volatile, oily substance developed in the coffee bean during roasting.

COLOMBIAN Straight coffee from Colombia.

COMMERCIAL COFFEES Pre-ground, pre-packaged (pre-brewed in the case of instant or soluble) coffees sold by brand name.

CONTINENTAL ROAST Coffee roasted dark brown, with a bittersweet tang.

CONTINUOUS ROASTER Large commercial coffee roasting apparatus which roasts coffee continuously, rather than in "batches."

COSTA RICAN Straight coffee from Costa Rica.

CÚCUTA A coffee grown in Colombia, but usually shipped through Maracaibo, Venezuela.

DARK FRENCH ROAST Coffee roasted nearly black.

DARK ROAST Coffee roasted darker than the North American norm.

DECAFFEINATED or CAFFEINE-FREE COFFEE Coffee roasted from whole beans which have had their caffeine removed in the green state.

DEMITASSE "Half-cup" in French; half-size, or 3-ounce cup.

DJIMMAH See Jimma.

DOMINICAN REPUBLIC Straight coffee from the Dominican Republic.

DRIP METHOD Brewing coffee by allowing hot water to settle down through a bed of ground coffee.

ECUADOR Straight coffee from Ecuador.

EL SALVADOR Straight coffee from El Salvador.

ESPRESSO A roast of coffee and a method of brewing.

ETHIOPIAN Straight coffee from Ethiopia; the kind generally sold in specialty stores is plantation-grown Harrar.

EUROPEAN PREPARATION A term sometimes used to describe coffee from which imperfect beans, pebbles, and other foreign matter have been removed by hand.

EUROPEAN ROAST Coffee roasted dark brown, with a bittersweet tang.

EXCELSO A grade of Colombian coffee.

EXTRA FINE Best grade of Venezuelan coffee.

FILTER METHOD Brewing coffee by any method in which water filters down through a bed of ground coffee.

FLAVOR What distinguishes the taste of a coffee once its acidity, body and aroma have been described.

FRENCH ROAST Coffee roasted dark brown, at times nearly black, with a bittersweet tang.

GOOD HARD BEAN A grade of Costa Rican coffee grown at altitudes of 3,300 to 3,900 feet.

GREEN COFFEE Unroasted coffee.

GUATEMALAN Straight coffee from Guatemala.

HAITIAN Straight coffee from Haiti.

HARD Trade term for low-quality coffee.

HARD BEAN High-grade, mountain-grown coffee from Central or South America, so called because the cool mountain temperatures produce a slowly matured, dense bean. Also grades of both Guatemalan and Costa Rican coffee.

HARRAR, HARAR, HARARI The most noted coffee of Ethiopia, grown on plantations near the ancient capital of Harrar.

HAWAIIAN Straight coffee from Hawaii. More commonly named Kona.

HEAVY ROAST Very dark-roasted coffee, with a bittersweet tang.

HEREDIA One of the better coffees of Costa Rica.

HIGH GROWN Arabica coffees grown at altitudes over 2,000 feet, usually higher. Such coffees are superior to coffees grown at lower altitudes. The term "high grown" also figures in many grade descriptions.

HIGH ROAST Coffee roasted slightly darker than the North American norm.

HUATUSCO, ALTURA HUATUSCO One of the better coffees from Veracruz State, Mexico.

INSTANT COFFEE More properly, soluble coffee. A convenience food made by rapidly dehydrating freshly brewed coffee.

ITALIAN ROAST Coffee roasted dark brown with a bittersweet tang.

JAMAICAN BLUE MOUNTAIN A fine, classically balanced coffee from the Wallensford Estate in Jamaica.

JAMAICAN HIGH MOUNTAIN Straight coffee grown in the mountains of Jamaica and exported under the market name "high mountain supreme."

JAVA Straight coffee from the island of Java, Indonesia.

JIMMA, DJIMMAH Coffee from southwestern Ethiopia, usually a naturally processed, wild coffee inferior to plantation-grown Harrar coffees.

WORDS FOR IT

JINOTEGA One of the better coffees of Nicaragua.

KALOSSI The best Celebes or Sulawesi coffee.

KENYA Straight coffee from Kenya. The best grade is AA.

KILIMANJARO Coffee from the slopes of Mt. Kilimanjaro in Tanzania.

KIVU Arabica coffee from Zaire grown near Rwanda-Burundi border.

KONA Straight coffee from the Kona (southwestern) coast of the island of Hawaii.

LIGHT FRENCH ROAST Coffee roasted slightly darker than the North American norm.

LIGHT ROAST Coffee roasted lighter than the North American norm.

LONGBERRY HARRAR Coffee grade from Ethiopia.

MAM Acronym for Medellín, Armenia, and Manizales, three of the most famous and best coffees of Colombia.

MANDHELING The most famous coffee from Sumatra.

MANIZALES One of the better coffees of Colombia.

MARACAIBO One of the best coffees of Venezuela.

MARAGOGIPE (Mah-rah-goh-shzee-peh) A variety of *Coffea arabica* which first appeared in Brazil, and has since been planted all over the world.

MATAGALPA One of the better coffees of Nicaragua.

MATTARI One of the best coffees of Yeman.

MBEYA Coffee from the south of Tanzania.

MEDELLÍN One of the best coffees of Colombia.

MEDIUM ROAST, MEDIUM HIGH ROAST Coffee roasted to standard North American tastes: medium brown.

MELIOR or PLUNGER-TYPE BREWER Melior is the brand name of a popular French brewer which separates spent grounds by forcing a filter down through the coffee.

MÉRIDA One of the best Venezuelan coffees; usually classed as a Maracaibo.

MEXICAN Straight coffee from Mexico.

MIDDLE EASTERN, "TURKISH" COFFEE Coffee ground to a powder, sweetened, brought to a boil and served grounds and all.

MILD A trade term for high-quality arabica coffees. Often contrasted with "hard," or inferior coffees.

MOCHA Straight coffee from the southwestern tip of the Arabian peninsula, present-day Yeman; named for the ancient port of Mocha. Also a drink combining chocolate and coffee.

MOCHA HARRAR Name for the peaberry grade of Harrar coffee from Ethiopia.

MOCHA-JAVA A blend of (usually) one part straight Arabian Mocha coffee and two parts straight Java Arabica. The world's oldest blend.

MOSHI Coffee from the slopes of Mt. Kilimanjaro in Tanzania.

MYSORE Straight coffee from Mysore, south central India.

NAIROBI Coffee from the slopes of Mt. Kenya in Kenya.

NATURALS, NATURAL-PROCESSED COFFEE Coffee processed by the "dry" method, in which the husk is removed from the bean after the coffee berries have been dried.

NEAPOLITAN MACCHINETTA A style of drip coffee brewer associated with Naples.

NEW ENGLAND ROAST Coffee roasted lighter than the North American norm.

NEW GUINEA Straight coffee from New Guinea.

NEW ORLEANS COFFEE Dark-roasted coffee blended with up to 40 percent chicory.

NICARAGUAN Straight coffee from Nicaragua.

OAXACA (Wah-*hah*-kuh) Straight coffee from the southern Mexican state of Oaxaca.

OCOA One of the better coffees of the Dominican Republic.

OPEN-POT COFFEE Coffee brewed by steeping (not boiling) ground coffee in an open pot.

ORIZABA, ALTURA ORIZABA One of the better coffees from Veracruz State, Mexico.

PARCHMENT One of the three skins of the coffee fruit, lying between the outer skin and the pulp and the innermost, or "silver" skin.

PEABERRY A small, round bean formed when only one bean develops at the heart of the coffee berry, rather than the usual two.

PERCOLATION Technically, any method of coffee brewing in which hot water percolates, or filters down through, a bed of ground coffee. More commonly refers to a coffee maker which utilizes the bubble power of boiling water to force water up a tube and over a bed of ground coffee.

PERGAMINO See Parchment.

PERUVIAN Straight coffee from Peru.

PRIMO LAVADO, PRIME WASHED A grade of Mexican coffee, which includes most of the fine coffees of Mexico.

PYROLYSIS The chemical breakdown, during roasting, of fats and carbohydrates into the delicate oils which provide all of coffee's aroma and most of its flavor.

QUAKERS Discolored or deformed coffee beans.

RANTEPAO Coffee from the island of Celebes or Sulawesi, Indonesia.

REGULAR ROAST Coffee roasted to North American tastes: medium brown.

RIOY A medicinal, iodine-like flavor in certain mass-harvested and processed coffee beans.

ROBUSTA, COFFEA ROBUSTA A botanical species of the genus *Coffea;* the only significant competitor to *Coffea arabica.* Robusta produces coffee of inferior quality, which is increasingly used as a basis for instant coffee blends.

SANANI One of the best coffees of Yeman.

SANTO DOMINGO Former name for Dominican Republic, and often still used to indicate that country's coffee.

SANTOS Coffee-growing region in southern Brazil, named after its principal port.

SHARKI One of the best coffees of Yeman.

SHORTBERRY HARRAR Coffee grade from Ethiopia.

SIDAMO Coffee from south central Ethiopia; inferior to plantation-grown Harrar coffees.

SPANISH ROAST Coffee roasted dark brown, with a bittersweet tang.

SPECIALTY COFFEE Custom whole-bean coffees sold in bulk by country of origin or roast.

STRAIGHT COFFEE An unblended coffee from a single country, region, and crop.

STRICTLY HARD BEAN The highest grade of Guatemalan and Costa Rican coffees.

STRICTLY HIGH GROWN Highest grade of El Salvador coffee.

STRICTLY HIGH GROWN WASHED Highest grade of Haitian coffee.

SULAWESI See Celebes.

SUMATRAN Straight coffee from Sumatra.

SUPREMO Finest grade of Colombian coffee.

TANZANIA Straight coffee from Tanzania, formerly Tanganyika.

TARRAZU One of the best and best-known coffees of Costa Rica.

TURKISH COFFEE See Middle Eastern coffee.

VACUUM METHOD A brewing method which differs from the filter method in that the boiling water is drawn through the ground coffee by means of a vacuum.

VENEZUELAN Straight coffee from Venezuela.

VIENNESE Describes either a coffee *roasted* slightly darker than usual, a *blend* of about two-thirds regular-roasted beans and one-third dark-roasted beans, or a coffee drink topped with whipped cream.

WASHED COFFEE Coffee prepared by the "wet" method, which involves removing the skin and pulp from the coffee bean while the berry is still moist. Most of the world's great coffees are processed by the wet method.

WHOLE BEAN Coffees which are roasted, but not yet ground.

YEMEN Straight coffee from Yemen. See Mocha.

YUNNAN Coffee from south China, near the Vietnam border.

SENDING FOR IT
A list of resources

The best place to buy your coffee, and most of your brewing gear, is at your neighborhood coffee specialty store. Look in the yellow pages under "Coffee Dealers—Retail" and "Gourmet Shops." If that fails I offer the following, which is not meant as a list of my favorite specialty coffee sellers, but rather as a selection of reliable coffee roasters who offer their wares through the mail. I wouldn't have space to list all the fine shops I've visited, and many I'd like to list, such as my friends at United Coffee Company in San Francisco, sell wholesale only.

ORDERING COFFEE THROUGH THE MAILS

If you buy a grinder and keep your whole-bean coffees sealed and *frozen (not* refrigerated), and grind a little at a time just before brewing, you can order up to about a month's supply at a time and always have reasonably fresh coffee. Your alternative is to buy a large quantity of green coffee, which keeps almost indefinitely, and roast your own.

Ground coffees will not keep well, however, even in the freezer, so if there is no specialty coffee store near and you don't buy a grinder, you might as well stash this book next to your college political science text and last year's best seller and buy some canned coffee.

All of the firms I list below welcome mail orders and promise prompt service and freshly roasted coffee. Write for order forms and latest prices.

Vancouver
Murchie's
560 Cambie Street
Vancouver, British Columbia V6B 2N7
Murchie's, an old, well-established importer/roaster, offers seven straight coffees and seven blends (but no caffeine-free coffees). Postage runs $1.25 and up for the United States.

Seattle
Starbucks
2010 Airport Way South
Seattle, Washington 98134
A conscientious roaster offering 11 straight coffees and 10 blends, including two decaffeinated. Phone orders accepted with Mastercharge and Visa. Packing charge is $1; sliding shipping charges; will ship by air.

San Francisco Bay Area
Peet's Coffee and Tea, Inc.
2124 Vine Street
Berkeley, California 94708
Of the many fine specialty roasters in the San Francisco Bay Area, I prefer Peet's, which offers a huge assortment of coffees. Their four caffeine-free blends include a water-only processed coffee.

Cunningham's
4050 Piedmont Avenue
Oakland, California 94611
Cunningham's offers a large selection of straight coffees and blends, and charges a sliding scale for shipping and handling.

Los Angeles
Polly's Gourmet Coffee
4606 East 2nd Street
Long Beach, California 90803
Polly's offers 21 straight coffees and five blends, and will custom-roast your choice of blend or straight coffee if you order five pounds or more of it. Two dollar shipping charge regardless of weight or destination.

San Diego
Pannikin
645 G Street
San Diego, California 92101
Pannikin sells 12 straight coffees, seven blends and three caffeine-free blends, and charges a sliding scale, from $2.50 to a maximum of $5.50, for postage and handling. Will accept payment through Visa and Master charge.

New York
Paprikás Weiss Importer
Dept. SF1
1546 Second Avenue
New York, New York 10028
Paprikás Weiss is a large gourmet foods and cookware concern; for a dollar you can get their catalogue, which not

only lists their coffees (eight straight coffees, seven blends, one caffeine-free blend, and one unspecified green coffee), but also hundreds of other foods and kitchen items, including a small assortment of coffee brewers and grinders. Their prices are high, however, and the postage and handling charge is $3.90, regardless of weight or destination.

Zabar's
2245 Broadway
New York, New York 10024
Zabar's is the Metropolitan Museum of delicatessens with bargain-basement prices. One of two authorized North American importers of the Wallensford Estate Blue Mountain coffee, Zabar's offered it in fall of 1980 for $6.98 a pound, an extraordinary price for this coffee. Zabar's also carries four additional straight coffees, six blends, a decaffeinated dark roast, and a water-only process decaffeinated. Minimum order is five pounds; 60 cents per pound shipping and handling.

Washington D.C.
M.E. Swing Co.
1013 E. Street, N.W.
Washington, D.C. 20004
A classic roaster from the pre-boutique era, Swing's offers a small but excellent selection of coffees at low prices. Their packing charge of 20 cents is more than reasonable, and they simply add UPS charges to your bill. No minimum order.

ORDERING ACCESSORIES
THROUGH THE MAILS
Small grinders and some brewers, like the Melitta and Chemex, are often available at small department stores, and large metropolitan department stores usually carry a wide range of coffee accessories, including exotic and imported gear. Another good place to look is the bamboo-furniture-and-incense-burner-type import store.

General Accessories
The best mail order selection of brewers and grinders I've come across is in the Pannikin brochure out of San Diego, but though Pannikin prices are fair they are no bargain. To save money, order from Zabar's in New York, whose selection is less complete but whose prices run 20 to 30 percent lower than most other suppliers. See above for addresses for Pannikan and Zabar's.

Grinders
Both Pannikin and Zabar's carry small blade grinders, the Braun burr mill, and the Spong hand wall mill. The Quaker City Hand Grain Grinder which I recommend so highly in Chapter 5 can be ordered directly from the manufacturer:
Nelson and Sons, Inc.
P.O. Box 1296
Salt Lake City, Utah 84110
It costs about $12 plus postage.
Zabar's most outrageous bargain is the Bosch K3 electric burr mill. Apparently a Zabar's special, this machine at $20 outperforms the similar Braun and

Krups mills, which retail for anywhere from $40 to $55. For passionate espresso fanciers, Zabar's also carries the sturdy, no-nonsense Olympia grinder at $135, and Faema Sales Corporation (see espresso brewers) the "Moka" at $65.

Filter brewers
See Pannikin and Zabar's, above. You can also order the excellent Melitta line of filter coffee makers, including their new automatic electric models, directly from:
Melitta Inc.
1401 Berlin Road
Cherry Hill, New Jersey 08003.

Espresso brewers
For smaller machines, see Pannikin and Zabar's, above. For the larger home machines see Zabar's or write to:
Faema Sales Corporation
450 West 44th Street
New York, New York 10036.
For bargain prices on the stovetop Atomic and the La Cara table top lever action machine, contact:
Thomas Cara
517 Pacific Avenue
San Francisco, California 94133.

Cold water brewers
Toddy Products Inc.
1206 Brooks Street
Houston, Texas 77009
The Toddy company offers its cold water brewer through the mail, postpaid, for $18.50 as of this writing.

INDEX

INDEX

BIOGRAPHICAL NOTES

KENNETH DAVIDS' vocation of writing and his avocation of coffee drinking inevitably culminated in this book. His fascination with coffee began in Europe in 1958; he admits to having spent much of his life since in coffee houses and cafés, drinking coffee, talking, and writing. Born in Chicago, Davids graduated from Northwestern University and later received his master's degree in English from the University of California at Berkeley. He has lived in Europe, Mexico, and Hawaii, his travels including several weeks spent among coffee roasters and fanciers in Great Britain preparing the British edition of this book. He eventually carried his love for cafés to the point of co-owning and managing one in Berkeley. At present he teaches and is Vice President for Instruction at California College of Arts and Crafts in Oakland. His other published works include translations from the Hawaiian language and a novel, *The Softness on the Other Side of the Hole,* published by Grove Press in 1968.

M. L. DUNIEC was born in Germany and raised in Longview, Washington. She received a bachelor of fine arts in printmaking at California College of Arts and Crafts and has taught art at Lower Columbia College in Washington. She is presently Art Director for Boysen Paint Company in Los Angeles.